YOU CAN'T
LOSE
THEM ALL

YOU CAN'T LOSE THEM ALL

TALES OF A DEGENERATE GAMBLER AND HIS RIDICULOUS FRIENDS

SAL IACONO

Foreword by Jimmy Kimmel

TWELVE

NEW YORK BOSTON

Twelve
Hachette Book Group
1290 Avenue of the Americas, New York, NY 10104
twelvebooks.com
twitter.com/twelvebooks

First edition: January 2021

Twelve is an imprint of Grand Central Publishing. The Twelve name and logo
are trademarks of Hachette Book Group, Inc.

The publisher is not responsible for websites (or their content) that are not
owned by the publisher.

The Hachette Speakers Bureau provides a wide range of authors for speaking
events. To find out more, go to www.hachettespeakersbureau.com or call
(866) 376-6591.

All photos courtesy of the author.

Library of Congress Cataloging-in-Publication Data

Names: Iacono, Sal, author.
Title: You can't lose them all : Tales of a degenerate gambler and his
    ridiculous friends / Sal Iacono.
Description: First edition. | New York : Twelve, 2021.
Identifiers: LCCN 2020030160 | ISBN 9781538735329 (hardcover) |
    ISBN 9781538735343 (ebook)
Subjects: LCSH: Iacono, Sal. | Gamblers—United States—Biography. |
    Television personalities—United States—Biography. | Gambling—Anecdotes. |
    Sports betting—Anecdotes.
Classification: LCC HV6710.3 .I23 2021 | DDC 795.092 [B]—dc23
LC record available at https://lccn.loc.gov/2020030160

ISBNs: 978-1-5387-3532-9 (hardcover), 978-1-5387-3534-3 (ebook)

Printed in the United States of America

LSC-C

Printing 2, 2021

*This book is dedicated to my sports gambling
brethren who have been unable to crack the magical
52.4 percent winning threshold required to beat the house.
I pray you've made up for it in drink tickets or,
like me, at the buffet.*

CONTENTS
A CHEATER'S GUIDE TO READING MY BOOK

Hi there. Thanks for purchasing this book.

Or if you're standing in a bookstore, just thumbing through the pages, keep moving, buddy, this isn't a library.

Anyhow, in honor of Bill Belichick and the New England Patriots, I offer this cheat sheet for getting to the stories you, my adoring fans and library loiterers, want to get to. So here we go...

FOREWORD

My cousin Sal (yes, he is my real cousin) is unlike anyone I've ever known. None of us can figure out how he happened. He misses nothing. His brain is a massive supercomputer jam-packed with memories long forgotten by everyone other than him. He is a mathematical wizard. He is a physical threat, with a trunk as hard as a pig's. He has wild impulses that he elects not to control. He relishes discomfort; he rolls around in it. He is prone to sudden acts of cartoonish violence. He wrestles strangers. For years he kept his toenails long to use as weapons. He eats room service left on the floor outside the doors of hotel rooms. He gets into car accidents on purpose. He'll offer you a ride home and intentionally drive for hours in the wrong direction. Once, when I was typing, he tiptoed in and touched the center of my back with his penis.

He is a lunatic. He ate a whole basket of shrimp tails. He is a completely unpredictable, nonstop instigator of nonsense. And yet, somehow, despite a record of consistently antisocial behavior, he is everyone's favorite coworker, person, and friend. The guy who randomly smashes a lamp on your desk or hangs up your phone when you've been on hold with your credit card company for forty-five minutes is the first guy you call when your mother dies (usually not his fault) or when you need a loan you know you'll never have to pay back.

He deliberately threw a coworker's aunt's camera in the garbage. That coworker invited him over for Christmas.

What makes Sal especially hard to figure out is his kindness, warmth, and generosity. These are qualities rarely seen in a maniac. Did I mention he is a doctor of jurisprudence? After he earned his degree at the prestigious Touro School of Law and Lawn Mowers, I convinced Sal to ditch his plan to practice real estate law and move to California to live and work with me in the lucrative world of local radio. What didn't seem like a wise decision then turned out to be one of the best decisions either of us ever made.

Sal has a totally original sense of humor. Every comment, every text, every email is a reminder that, day after day, no one is funnier. The jokes go deep. He makes you laugh all the way to your bones. The characters he surrounds himself with and cares for are almost as hard to explain as he is. To call it a motley crew would result in a lawsuit from the Motleys. They are his Island of Misfit Toys. The stories you are about to read are true. Some of the names have been changed, but no one is innocent.

—Cousin Jimmy Kimmel

THE FALL OF TROJANOWSKI

Tony B: If I get you the phone number, will you ask her to the wedding?
Me: Sure. Go for it.

Before we get into my stories about the seedy underworld of gambling, here's a story about how I met my wife. A risky adventure that led to the only real sure thing in my life.

Back in the spring of 1999, my friends were throwing our buddy Donick a bachelor party in Mexico. The plan was to rent a mansion in the hills of Puerto Vallarta. I didn't drink, so I would watch my pals guzzle tequila all weekend and, at the same time, pray the satellite dish would kick in so I could see the Final Four game between Duke and Michigan State.

I had very little money back then but somehow was able to bid $8,000 on Duke on credit in what is referred to as a

"Calcutta pool." This is where a bunch of people bid on teams and you get money for every round your squad advances in the NCAA tournament. As a result, Coach K's team reaching the Final Four was a good thing for me.

So a bunch of us flew to Mexico for a weekend of debauchery. Puerto Vallarta is beautiful and the fellas got hammered and I was able to watch a scrambled signal of the game on satellite. Elton Brand dominated and the hated Blue Devils made the finals, which meant I was guaranteed to make money off of money I didn't have.

Isn't this a romantic story so far?

An even better call was heading out with the bachelor party later that evening to a local bar called Carlos O'Brian's (a name we would later bestow on our family mutt).

It was a wonderful scene. A bunch of well-to-do Hollywood dudes buying shots for the rest of the bar, which happened to be made up of mostly attractive women. My friend Daniel was handing out lemon shots; Adam Carolla was getting recognized as the host of his popular MTV show *Loveline*. My cousin Jimmy was there, and—having given Adam his start in show business—this was an ironic scenario where Adam was getting celebrity love and Jimmy wasn't. Suddenly, after a solid hour of Jimmy being ignored, a beautiful young woman in a red dress approached him.

Beautiful young woman in a red dress: Wait—are you the guy on *Win Ben Stein's Money*?
Jimmy: Yes, I am.
Beautiful young woman in a red dress: Oh...my father watches that show.

Everyone laughs at Jimmy.

She didn't realize what a back-handed burn she had just delivered. We all had a good laugh about it, and I knew right away that this was the woman I would spend the rest of the evening with. Melissa Trojanowski was on spring break with her friends from Wisconsin. With a name like Trojanowski, there was only about a 170 percent chance she would hail from the Dairy State. After making small talk with her, I found out that Trojanowski was a grad student at Madison staying with her two friends in a Hyatt in the heart of Puerto Vallarta. I barely got this information out of her before my friend Daniel announced that he was rounding up several groups from the bar to come party with us back at the house. In a master stroke of debauchery, Daniel lined up a bunch of cabs, loaded groups of women into them, and shifted the festivities to the rented mansion.

Trojanowski and I continued our conversation there and even played tennis on the mansion's outdoor court. I didn't let her win, mainly because I'm a competitive idiot, but she didn't seem to mind and, in fact, apologized for hitting the ball into the net for most of the match.

I liked her more and more as the evening went on and even managed to sneak a kiss in when no one was looking. Eventually, Trojanowski and her friends left and that, I felt, was that.

Jimmy and my buddies were annoyed with me.

"How did you not get Trojanowski's phone number?"

"You finally meet a woman who is not repulsed by you and you just let her go?"

The way I saw it, I lived in California, she lived in Wisconsin. I had just had a miserable time wrapping up a long-distance relationship and didn't have the stamina to start up another one. I'd be satisfied getting to first base with a nice lady every few years in a foreign country.

Fortunately, us not being meant to be wasn't meant to be.

A couple months later my friend Matt Silverstein, one of the *Man Show* writers, was getting married in Chicago.

That's when my good pal Tony approached me with the bet.

"If I find her phone number, will you take her to the wedding?"

Seemed like not a lot of downside to this bet, so I agreed.

All we knew was Trojanowski's last name and the fact that she attended grad school at Madison. The Internet was fairly new, so without Facebook or Instagram this was going to be a wild-badger chase.

Somehow, Tony got in touch with the university and used his magic powers to convince the bursar, or whoever, to give him the phone number. That number was then placed on my desk about twenty minutes after the "bet" was made.

Milwaukee was a cheese block's throw from Chicago, so this could actually happen. I called Trojanowski and told her that I wasn't stalking her—always a solid way to begin a conversation—and invited her to the wedding, which was a few weeks away. She seemed weirded out and said she'd get back to me later in the week.

I figured I was a 7/1 long shot at this point. This bet was one well-timed excuse away from being bust. Anything would've worked. The smart money was on "Sorry, I forgot my uncle Ray is playing lead accordion at the local polka festival that night."

Much to my surprise, Trojanowski didn't wait a few days but actually called back in a few hours. "I would love to go to the wedding" was not what I was expecting. I was stunned.

So we went to the wedding, had a great time, and proceeded to alternate flying to each other's hometowns one weekend a month for a year until she graduated with a master's in social work and agreed to settle down with me in my cousin Jimmy's basement. (I know: How?...Why?)

Melissa Trojanowski was everything I could want in a wife and more. I popped the question and she agreed to walk down the aisle to the Fox NFL Sunday theme song.

She knew that gambling and my love for sports were a tremendous part of my life. We honeymooned in Kauai where every morning I'd run downstairs to the business center of the hotel to check on Asian soccer scores. I had a theory that I would profit if I parlayed seven or eight big favorites together to get even money. Yup, this on my honeymoon. The theory, by the way, proved to be faulty.

Now, that kind of behavior would've urged almost any other woman to seek an annulment. Not Trojanowski. She took everything in stride.

A couple years after my Asian soccer parlay phase—which ended up being a losing proposition, believe it or not—we planned on having our first child. Anyone who's been through this knows there can be a lot of preparation involved. The mother-to-be has to figure out when she's ovulating. She has to pee on a stick to see if she's pregnant. In solidarity, I would also pee on a stick, by the shed in the backyard. I figured either we were in this together or we weren't.

We were in full baby-making mode in the fall of 2004. At the same time I was starring in hidden camera comedy bits for *Jimmy Kimmel Live!* We'd shoot these in Las Vegas, because, at the time, the state of Nevada deemed it legal if one party had knowledge of the recordings. Another reason Nevada is the greatest state in the universe.

We would typically camp out at my friend Ken's house and screw with delivery people. It was an absolute blast. Didn't seem like work at all. We made people set up bouncy houses in the living room, had pizza delivery guys participate in wrestling matches, asked locksmiths to help me break into a safe, and so on. A two-day shoot would yield seven or eight comedy bits.

That particular week I shot in Vegas on Thursday and Friday and planned to stay through Saturday night to attend the Oscar De La Hoya–Bernard Hopkins fight at the MGM. I bet a lot of money on Hopkins (a 2-to-1 favorite) and figured it's always more fun to lose in person.

As I was finishing up the hidden camera bits on Friday, I get a call from Melissa. (She had mercifully ditched the Trojanowski name at this point.)

"Come home, I'm ovulating."

An interesting surprise. Back at the turn of the century, you couldn't find out if you were ovulating by asking Siri. You had to make your own fertility calendar out of beets.

It was a pain in the ass to get back to Los Angeles on such short notice, especially with my weekend plans, but you can't just take months off from the pregnancy quest, so I jumped on a Southwest flight and met Melissa at an Outback Steakhouse by the Burbank airport. After sharing a Bloomin' Onion and Kookaburra Wings, we made relations in our bed, then I jumped on a plane and flew back to Las Vegas to witness Bernard Hopkins KO De La Hoya with a kidney punch.

This frantic fertility quest worked out. Nine months later we had our first son. As far as names went, we could've gone with

Oscar or Bernard to pay tribute to the fight. Or maybe throw Outback Steakhouse a bone. "Barbie" or "Ribeye" Iacono kind of had a ring to it. Instead, we got lazy, breezed through the A's in the book, and settled on Archie, which happens to be the name of my favorite TV character of all time: Archie Bunker.

One month into Archie Iacono's life, I was scheduled to appear on *Jimmy Kimmel Live!* for my birthday to present a hidden camera bit I had shot at a jewelry store.

When I got to the couch, Jimmy surprised me by introducing my childhood crush pop star Debbie Gibson. I was infatuated with Debbie Gibson as a sixteen-year-old. Try as I might, I just couldn't shake…her love. Debbie's poster hung in my room right next to Genesis, Rowdy Roddy Piper, and Huey Lewis and the News. That was my pubescent Mount Rushmore.

Debbie grew up a few towns over from me and was the same age. I remember going to the Jones Beach Theater with my friend Allison to see her in concert. We had the worst seats. Our backs were literally against the back wall. I brought a sign that said "Kiss Me, Debbie—It's My Birthday." So corny, but it actually didn't matter, since being in the last row in the upper deck, Allison and I were the only ones who could see the sign.

And now here we were, twenty-eight years later to the day, and Debbie Gibson was singing "Lost in Your Eyes" while gazing into mine. It was a ridiculous scene. I thought it would be funny to just get up and leave, but I felt bad that she had come all the way out to do this, so I stayed and let the embarrassment rush over me.

A few miles away, Melissa was watching the East Coast ABC feed at home. She was super-hormonal, having just given birth to Archie, and was very upset about this faux birthday date.

But as part of my birthday gift and because she's a great lady, Melissa didn't let me know until years later how upset she was. Debbie probably wasn't thrilled with it, either.

When our second child was born, I bugged Melissa to come up with a silly name. We both liked Jack for a first name and I had the idea of Tripper for his middle name. What a way to honor John Ritter, the late great comedic actor. Ritter played Jack Tripper on *Three's Company.* He had passed away a few years earlier and was widely known as one of the nicest guys to ever step foot in Hollywood, let alone the Regal Beagle.

"Jack Tripper Iacono" had a ring to it, but not a ring my wife was fond of. (At this point she was skeptical about the one on her finger, too.)

So we went with my backup plan: "Jack Romo Iacono." Cowboys quarterback Tony Romo was my adult idol. It's weird: I have a problem with anyone over thirty-five years old wearing a jersey with a current player's name on it, but naming your kid after someone younger than you? Totally fine. Besides, Romo hadn't won anything. I figured it's easy to name your son after Joe Montana or Wayne Gretzky, but an athlete might be extra-inspired to achieve greatness if he or she hears people are saddling their spawn with their name. Melissa reluctantly agreed and we went with Jack Romo.

Melissa Reluctantly Agreed should've been the title of this book.

Melissa has witnessed me pull out my gambling tally sheet tens of thousands of times during meals, recitals, communions, bar mitzvahs, funerals, and any inappropriate time you can imagine.

She has endured me bringing a miniature TV to her best

friend's wedding. To my credit I kept it hidden underneath our table, illuminating the room so that all in attendance could only surmise that there was a spaceship landing by our feet.

She has handled my gift for flatulence with dignity and tolerance.

She has dealt with my insane family for more than twenty years. From cutting my father's toenails to wiping my autistic sister's rear end, caring for the Iaconos has not been a walk in the park by any means.

And she lets it all slide with a head shake and a smile that could brighten up a Malaysian cave.

Melissa Trojanowski is an absolute saint—and not the kind that cost me $28,750 by blowing the 2019 NFC championship game. The holy kind.

The only thing I did right by her was allow her to change that horrible last name. Aside from that, I don't deserve her. It might be the case that no one does. She's a −10,000,000,000,000 lock to advance to heaven. And that's the easiest bet there is.

BEST PLACE TO MEET YOUR WIFE

CUSTOMER RECEIPT

On spring break in Mexico
(2/1)
Library (4/1)
Church (7/1)
NRA rally (300/1)

Win total:

Total bet:

65988 - 4 4807802443545 379045345- 3 678 4534 3 -4 678 678353 678534

LA DOLCE VITA

When it comes to one-on-one wagers with me, nothing is off-limits. I even bet my editor how many copies of this book I could sell. That's not a joke. I wagered under 13,500 copies sold. That way, if I "win," I can say "I told you so." In fact, your purchase of this memoir could cause me to lose yet again. So thanks a lot for that.

I've bet on baseball, basketball, hockey, wrestling (pro and amateur), hot dog–eating contests, horse races, dog races, bird races, presidential elections, all levels of football—including my eight-year-old son's flag league and, of course, the Puppy Bowl. I've wagered on tennis, soccer, golf, and every type of award show that anyone has rented a tuxedo for. Not to mention reality shows like *Dancing with the Stars*. I've risked as much money on Drew Lachey as I have Drew Brees. So, yes, it's a problem, spread through all genres of life.

But that doesn't stop people from asking me what my worst beat or the most money that I lost as a gambler was. I think it makes them feel better about themselves to hear the answer.

It's weird: most human beings know that it's inappropriate to ask a drug addict for their best overdose story, but for some reason the idea of a powerless person losing everything he has on a game of chance is amusing. I actually agree—it is. And the short answer to what my worst loss was entirely depends on how much it hurt. The pain index relies on several factors.

Take the 2019 NFC Championship game, for instance. It was during that contest that I squandered the most I ever bet on a football game (legally) in the final moments, when a Rams defensive back wasn't called for pass interference after mauling a Saints wide receiver, like, seven seconds before the ball arrived. It was an atrocious noncall—so bad that the following season they changed the rule to allow instant replay of pass interference noncalls. But I still had a little money left over to buy my spawn a burrito at Chipotle, so it could've been worse.

Let's compare that to when I was eight years old and flipping baseball cards on the playground at Connolly Elementary School in Glen Cove, New York. I lost one hundred cards (every other third grader would risk five max) to the local bully, who figured a way to cheat and steal from my pile when I wasn't paying attention. It was all I had and I wasn't getting them back even if I had Mets slugger Dave Kingman himself bang down the little thug's door with a Louisville Slugger. So, in a way, that was my worst and most hurtful beat with many more in my future.

Over the last forty years I have shared "betting experiences" with doctors, lawyers, teachers, agents, bookies, writers, comedians, podcasters, radio DJs, TV producers, baseball players, front-office executives, bandleaders, movie stars, publicists, weed lab owners, hedge fund operators, and even professional wrestlers. My intention is to detail many of these interactions without getting sued.

The more I think about it, I was destined to be a gambler. The deck was stacked against me.

My parents named me Sal Iacono. I was born in Brooklyn. Sal Iacono from Brooklyn was not going to grow up to become curator of a museum. It just wasn't happening.

Sure, I tried to buck the trend by graduating from law school, but it didn't amount to anything, as I failed the bar exam twice. (The over/under was 1.5. I won that bet with myself too...kinda.) After twenty years, I just now paid off my student loans, so maybe I won't count that as a win.

● ● ●
● ● ●

I was named Sal Iacono after my father's father and am very proud of this distinction.

Grandpa Sal was a unique soul. Everyone who met him loved him dearly. Friends and family happily endured three-thousand-mile bus trips just to visit Grandpa Sal. He made you feel good being around him. Like most grandparents who grew up in the early 1900s, Grandpa Sal didn't have a ton of schooling but was wise beyond his education and, most charmingly, shared this wisdom with childlike exuberance.

Aside from being a kind soul, Grandpa Sal was the funniest guy any of us ever knew. I don't think I'll get an argument when I say every bit of our sense of humor comes from him. He was a tour de force at family gatherings and mastered even the most subtle forms of comedy. You know that game when you tap someone on the shoulder and try to get them to look?

He never once looked up. Undefeated in that stupid game. The most subtle tug of his shirt couldn't persuade Grandpa Sal to turn. In fact, in an attempt to further mock the tapper, after you attempted to make him look—he would tilt his head up and gaze at the sky. It doesn't seem like a great feat, but imagine never once getting fooled by the shoulder tap!

As far as practical jokes went, Grandpa Sal was the GOAT. Even the unplanned pranks ended up being pranks. He was in his eighties when he jumped in my aunt Joan and uncle Jimmy's pool. Everything seemed fine until he lay facedown for a few seconds...then motionless. A signature move he would employ for fun. My uncle Jimmy, in his work attire, jumped in to save him. As he pulled him out of the water and turned him over to breathe, Grandpa Sal spit water in his face. That was one of the few times anyone ever got mad at him.

OK, here's another one. At a wedding he once "helped" his wife, my grandma Edith, with her coat as they were set to leave. He draped it over her back, at the same time dropping a dozen knives and forks to make it look as if she were trying to steal from the catering hall. "Ah, Eda...why do you have to steal? We got plenty of this stuff at home."

He had the greatest one-liners, too. Whenever we celebrated his birthday, he would snuff out the candles on his cake with his gigantic golden glove–experienced hands. One by one he'd pinch out the flames while everyone was screaming at him, then turn to us with a smile on his face and whisper, "Call the ambulance!"

That smile was unforgettable. So many grumpy grandpas out there. Not this one. He'd literally fall asleep with a grin on his face. This was even more impressive considering he had to suffer through pain in the same rib he'd somehow repeatedly break over and over for all of the twenty-nine years I was privileged to know him. I don't know: maybe in the grand scheme of things it was a bad idea for the family to have chipped in to buy him a moped for his seventy-fifth birthday.

In addition to the golden glove boxer thing, Grandpa Sal was great with his hands. He spent his grown-up years as an upholsterer while also working in a film lab. Then, when he retired, he'd paint famous people—usually local celebrities who appeared in TV ads—and family members' likenesses on eyeglass lenses that he collected and the insides of beer cans. I realize this is bizarre, even by grandfather standards, especially since he wasn't a big beer drinker and pretty much relied on the same pair of reading glasses for the better part of a half century. But it kept him busy and happy so we never questioned it. We also never questioned when he wore my grandmother's dentures until he died.

Grandpa had bigger projects as well. Much to the family's chagrin, Grandpa Sal once invented a device that would turn your television into a projection device, or "mechanism," as he loved to explain. The idea was you'd place this cockamamie magnifying glass over the television set and it would blow up the projected image on the nearest wall.

The only problem was, in order to take advantage of this invention, you had to be willing to pull the tube out of your TV and turn it upside down, and none of the grown-ups in the family were willing to offer their twenty-one-inch Zeniths as guinea pigs.

My cousin Jimmy and I did invert a spare television while no one was looking, and I have to say: it kind of worked as we watched the enlarged projection on Jimmy's bedroom ceiling. But that masterpiece didn't land him a job at Caltech. It just served as a fun project he could drive everyone crazy with—which I kind of think was the point. Creating bizarre and sometimes infuriating works of art was how he was going to live out his golden years. And then something miraculous happened.

In 1975 my uncle Frank, a retired police officer, inexplicably moved my aunt Chippy and my three cousins Ann, Sally, and Micki from Brooklyn to Las Vegas. Uncle Frank, a fun-loving man who later served as my cousin Jimmy's television sidekick, was very impulsive, and the move came out of nowhere. No one in our family ever left Brooklyn. I mean, it was the only place in the country where streaking down your apartment hallway while bringing trash to the incinerator was acceptable. Why take a chance anywhere else?

But Uncle Frank did it, and, interestingly enough, my grandparents followed. This was a really nice change of pace for my grandfather, who was now introduced to a town that specialized in hard-core gambling. As a New Yorker, maybe he'd bet on a horse or two, but I'm not sure he had a passion for horse racing; it was more something little old Italian men were supposed to do while chewing on a De Nobili cigar.

But Las Vegas was a different story. Now if he wanted to hide from everyone screaming at each other, he could take the bus downtown and gamble all day. Grandpa didn't have a lot of money, but he would make $20 last a good eight hours—and that included splurging for the senior citizen lunch special at the Silver Nugget.

Keno was his game. He'd take the pen and run over his

favorite numbers—birthdays, anniversaries—much like everyone else does. But his casino play really jumped to another level when he moved to slot machines, because when it came to the one-armed bandit, Grandpa Sal had a system.

He would approach a machine where the jackpot was one line off from where the wheels were in the rest position. So if an unattended slot machine had three jackpots on the top line instead of the desired middle line, he claimed it as his own. Once he settled in at that machine, he had a process for the physical pull. He would yank on the one-armed bandit, but only partially—never all the way down. When it didn't work, which was always, he'd explain to his detractors that he wasn't doing it right. This is what he did all day long. And then he'd go home and watch Letterman and paint on more eyeglass lenses and beer cans until he fell asleep.

WHAT A GODDAMN LIFE!

Pound for pound, Grandpa Sal was the greatest guy I've ever met. Forgive me if later in this book I say that about someone else. It's probably because I owe them money or something. But, honestly, Grandpa Sal was a legendary force in my life and a true inspiration to family men everywhere. Grandpa Sal would take complimentary pictures at Binion's Horseshoe, which featured a case holding $1 million. Whenever relatives would come to Vegas, he'd bring them downtown to pose with him. He has hundreds of these pictures. I think it made him feel rich, but I can tell you he didn't need it: with the love of everyone who knew him, he was the richest man to moped the planet.

From ages sixty-seven to ninety-two, Grandpa Sal truly lived la dolce vita—the sweet life—in Las Vegas. The moral of the story is it's never too late to start gambling. You'll see in the next couple hundred or so pages that I have great difficulty figuring out the moral to these stories. This serves as the perfect example.

BANNED FROM BINGO

I'd be remiss if I didn't also credit my grandmother for my degenerate ways. My father's mother was a simple old Italian woman. She had gigantic arms and an even bigger heart. Actually, I'm not going to lie. The arms were bigger. I used to laugh when Hulk Hogan would brag about his twenty-four-inch pythons. Grandma Edith's biceps had him beat by half a foot easy.

Like most Italian grandmothers, Edith Iacono showed her love through cooking. She was a culinary ninja and a literal one, given the proper motivation. Legend has it that Grandma Edith could stir gravy with one hand and discipline misbehaving children with another. And aside from nailing all Italian cuisine, my grandmother mastered fried chicken. Much like the modern-day Popeyes restaurant videos you see on YouTube, the grandchildren used to gather in the kitchen to brawl over the first helping of Grandma Edith's fried chicken.

For fun, Grandma Edith would watch *Joker's Wild* and *Family*

Feud while doing chores. She thought it was endearing that, before asking the families what they thought the survey said, host Richard Dawson would greet all of the female contestants with a kiss. In today's spectrum of unnecessary sexual advances, Dawson's full on lip locks would put him squarely between Louis C.K. and Bill Cosby. When my grandmother wasn't cooking or watching creepy game show hosts hit on contestants and their sisters, she liked to play *Pac-Man* on Atari. She'd sit in a La-Z-Boy gobbling power pellets for hours. Truth be told, most of the time she wasn't actually playing. Grandma would get so frustrated when she lost that my cousins Jimmy, Micki, and I thought it was best to alternate playing for her without her knowledge. She'd control the Player 2 joystick (which was inactive) and we would control the joystick that was actually plugged into the Atari console. Sometimes it was so obvious that she wasn't playing that you could actually catch Blinky and Inky rolling their eyes. But it was for the best, as the high scores brought her a sense of joy.

Yes, *Pac-Man* was a good short-term fix, but—like most Italian grandmothers from the East Coast—Grandma Edith's true decades-long addiction was...you got it: bingo!

In her adult years, Grandma Edith played at any church that offered it, and when she and my grandfather moved to Las Vegas, it was game on. Unlimited bingo for my grandmother was like unlimited leg humping for a dog. She would play any chance she got, and when she was in charge of watching her grandchildren, she'd just bring us along.

We would each get one card to place our plastic chips on while Grandma Edith would oversee about two dozen bingo boards. She was like an air traffic controller in charge of a fleet of 747s. To this day, I still don't know how she was able to stay on top of that many bingo boards. But she did it. She never missed a number and would even fill in yours when you were dozing off.

And when it came to the "specials," she was just as prolific. The specials were paper versions of the board. You had to pay an extra ten cents a page for them, I think. Every bingo addict would load up on the specials because they paid out more than the regular games. Unlike the cardboard variety, the paper specials often had a gimmick. Instead of across or diagonally, you could be asked to create an X or hit all four corners or fill the entire card.

But the best part about the paper specials was the bingo markers. We, the grandkids, had a lot of fun marking each other up from head to toe. It was almost impossible to get the marks off. Mike Tyson would have an easier time removing his eye tattoo using a nail file than trying to erase the ink scars made by the bingo markers.

My grandmother would try to ignore this, as you can only pay attention to so many things at one time. She was intent on winning, and when she did, she'd call out "BINGO!" with the urgency of an armless man who had fallen in the shallow end of a pool at Caesars Palace.

After a win was claimed—the bingo caller would yell over to the verifier, who walked over to the potential winner. It was written in the bingo bible that this verifier had to be either of Italian or Jewish descent and at least 119 years old.

Bingo caller: Saul, in the back...
Saul: 13, 19, 41, 49, 56.
Bingo caller: That's a bingo.

And then Saul would pay the winner upwards of $25, and

everyone at the table would get to touch the money for good luck. This seemed to fly in the face of the competitive nature of bingo. Almost like Yankees slugger Aaron Judge letting the Red Sox use his bat after a grand slam. But I guess it was nice.

Everything about it was nice—too nice for our liking. My cousin Jimmy and I decided to jazz up the experience by screaming "Bingo!" at inopportune times—like when we didn't actually have bingo. We'd call it out after, like, three numbers, drawing the ire of every salty senior citizen in the room. I remember getting shushed and driving my grandmother, not to mention poor Saul, crazy. She gave us the death stare and then eventually would hold our hands down and explain in a low and terrifying voice, "You think this is funny, but when the bingo commission hears of it, you're going to be in trouble."

To be honest, I was a lot more fearful of Grandma Edith's wooden spoon than I was of the bingo commission. I mean, who were these losers and why did they have to form a commission? Also, what the hell were they going to do to us?

"Your disruptions have left us no other choice... You are banned from bingo."

Ouch. What will I ever do without bingo? Keep your dumb boards and chips. I should be home playing Atari anyway.

In retrospect, I probably shouldn't have been such a shitty kid. I should've kept my mouth shut and filled out the cards and appreciated what was being offered: a look into the wonderful world of gambling.

As for Grandma, sadly, she is gone. In 1984 she died of a headache, and I can now say without reservation that today I would do anything, including sitting through one month's worth of bingo and Richard Dawson, for a helping of her fried chicken.

FAVORITE GRANDMA MEALS

CUSTOMER RECEIPT

Fried chicken (2/1)

Escarole, beans, and polenta (5/2)

Ice tea with the spoon in the pitcher (25/1)

Burned eggs (300/1)

Win total: _____

Total bet: _____

65988 - 4 4807802443545 379045345- 3 678 4534 3 -4 678 678353 678534

A CHIP OFF THE OLD BLOCK

In my family, there are different levels of gambling addiction. I am at the top, my aunt Chippy is just behind me. Or maybe ahead. I'll let you decide after this chapter.

I've mentioned in earlier chapters my grandparents' zest for a jackpot, but when it comes to Iacono family lineage, my aunt Chippy really has the eye of the tigress and the mouth of a hippopotamus.

Aunt "Chippy," birth name Concietta, is my father's older sister, which was enough of a reason to be scared of her. When I was young I was deathly afraid of three entities: the Penguin from Batman, serial killer David Berkowitz (aka the Son of Sam), and my aunt Chippy. And not necessarily in that order. Aunt Chippy was a lovable figure who seemingly yelled at everyone she came across. The milkman. Her hairdresser. The church pastor. Didn't matter. She hollered at everyone at decibels AC/DC would be envious of. It's not her fault, really. She was born loud. Even when she complimented you, she screamed:

"OH, I LOVE YOUR HAIRCUT, SAL. YOU LOOK LIKE A BOY NOW. ANN, DOESN'T HE LOOK LIKE A BOY NOW? I'M SO HAPPY YOU GOT RID OF THOSE FRIGGIN' CURLS. THEY SHOULD BE BURIED IN THE SEWER FOREVER!!"

She was loud and brash and feared by most of her nieces and nephews and pretty much all of Brooklyn. When I was five years old, I was in my Aunt Joan's backyard in Brooklyn and decided to take the opportunity to show my cousin Sally, Aunt Chippy's daughter, my penis. Sally and I were both named after my grandfather Sal, and that seemed as good a reason as any to present my tiny unit. Sally shrieked and immediately threatened to tell her mother. The thought of an angry Aunt Chippy confronting me was the worst possible thing imaginable.

Sally ran into the house and locked the door behind her. I followed and began pounding on the glass, screaming and crying. Eventually the glass gave in and shattered, with a few shards sticking in my hand. My tiny pecker was still exposed as my fingers bled all over the concrete porch.

I vividly remember getting stitches in my fingers and ultimately being rewarded by my parents with a soundtrack album for a forgettable Eddie Albert movie, *Escape to Witch Mountain*—which happened to be my favorite at the time.

Sally, on the other hand, received a minor beating at the hands of Aunt Chippy for "causing" the incident.

That's how justice was dished out in our family. And as we got older, Aunt Chippy became less scary and was seen as more of a comedic figure. My cousin Jimmy's family now lived near her in Vegas, so he was able to focus his efforts on driving her completely out of her mind.

In order to do this, he needed to study Aunt Chippy like a lab mouse. At one family get-together we recorded an interaction between Chippy and her husband, my uncle Frank. This was back when Heinz ketchup first came out with the squeeze bottles.

Uncle Frank (banging on the bottle): Chip, how do you pour this?

Aunt Chippy: Oh, my God. Let me see. Frank, first you shake it. No, not like that. Turn it upside down. (Pause) Frank, do you have it opened? Frank, you gotta open it before it'll GODDAMN COME OUT! For crying out loud. He's so stupid, it's pathetic. My husband. He'll never invent a spaceship. He'll never invent an "aero"-plane. We're lucky that he knows how to ride in one.

It doesn't seem like much of an argument, as Uncle Frank merely asked an innocent question. Yet it was an exchange that the nieces and nephews have committed to memory for four decades. I put this homemade comedy tape up against Pryor, Carlin, and all the greats.

The angrier Aunt Chippy was, the more license we took to torture her. Jimmy led the charge in a big way. Between prank calls and putting loads in her cigarettes—one blew up in her boss's office—when it came to harassing Aunt Chippy, nothing was off-limits.

But it wasn't until I was about thirteen that I appreciated Aunt Chippy for an addiction other than yelling and smoking: video poker. She and my grandmother enjoyed bingo in

Brooklyn, but when they moved to the desert, my aunt Chippy truly found video poker to be her calling.

The great and terrible thing about video poker is its accessibility. In Las Vegas you can find a video poker machine in a 7-Eleven. This is not a joke. You could actually be fighting off a Slurpee brain freeze while deciding whether or not to draw three cards in pursuit of a flush. It wasn't uncommon for people to lose their nest egg—in Aunt Chippy's case, a cop's pension—in a bowling alley without ever having to change shoes.

At thirteen, I was playing video poker on a handheld version and had "won" enough to think I was good at it. So I decided that video poker with Aunt Chippy was going to be a major pit stop on my summer pilgrimage to Vegas.

Vegas is great, but it's not "We even let thirteen-year-olds play video poker" great. There were certain rules that needed to be followed—namely, the one where I had to stand thirty feet behind Aunt Chippy while she was playing. This mandatory separation was good, as it created distance between me and her Marlboro lights. On the other hand, it was challenging to figure out how to signal her without anyone noticing. But I couldn't let anything distract me. I gave Aunt Chippy $20 of my hard-earned *Newsday* paper route money, and the plan was for her to turn it into tens of millions of dollars. I was then going to take my new fortune and use it to purchase the Nassau Coliseum and sit wherever I wanted for Islanders games and WWF events. It all seemed like a very manageable plan.

Here's how we would pull it off. Aunt Chippy would be dealt a hand and then turn around, and I would discreetly signal which of the five cards to keep. If I held up two and then three fingers, that would mean keep the second and third and discard the rest.

After a few minutes the signaling became tedious. Aunt Chippy became impatient and I just started yelling instructions extra loud over the sound of crashing bowling pins.

We did well. We hit a couple of full houses and a four-of-a-kind. I was up $80 when Aunt Chippy offered rare sage advice: "We're done now. We're going to just walk away."

She said this in a low voice, which was more hurtful than anything she had ever screamed at the top of her lungs. We were kicking the crap out of this machine. Why would we quit now?

She further explained: "I've seen it a million times. People get up, they keep playing, they lose more money than they have. We had a nice time. You won. Be happy and walk away."

I fully understood. When she said "people," she meant herself. It was good advice. This was her idea of a valuable lesson.

$80 meant I fell far short of my plans to own the Nassau Coliseum. Now I was going to have to wait in line like everyone else to buy tickets to see the Magnificent Muraco wrestle the Junkyard Dog. But deep down I knew she was right.

The main takeaway was I had the gambling bug. Had I lost the $80, maybe today I wouldn't be wearing makeup on television every day and talking about English Premier League over/unders. Perhaps I'd be a veterinarian or an elevator repairman. Or probably just a veterinarian or elevator repairman with a gambling problem.

Nowadays Aunt Chippy's gambling problem takes a backseat to her gullibility. In recent years a TV show budget has afforded my cousin Jimmy and me to play elaborate pranks on her.

A few years back, we had non–English-speaking "workers" paint her house orange and green. Jimmy was on the phone with me as I set up camp a few houses away, instructing Mexican actors to continue painting as they were getting threatened by a furious

Aunt Chippy. Things almost got physical when they began painting her shrubs. Jimmy sent me in to break up a near melee, at which point she slapped every part of my body three hundred times.

Aunt Chippy made the mistake one Easter of telling Jimmy that the arts and crafts class around the corner was her "one safe haven." We decided to change that. A few weeks later we hired an actor—in this case, the great Judo Gene LeBell—to sign up for and ruin the class. I stood behind the class, instructing Gene by walkie-talkie to screw with her mercilessly. Of the two hundred or so hidden camera bits I've participated in, this is my all-time favorite. With assistance from me in his earpiece, which was easily disguised as a hearing aid, Gene kept bragging that his nephew was a Las Vegas county commissioner. Aunt Chippy wasn't having it. She also wasn't having it when Judo Gene put sardines on her pottery dish, which was not yet dry from painting, or when he took his pants off after spilling margarita mix on them. Moments before she committed an assault on Gene, I stepped in. Aunt Chippy was relieved to see me and showed it in that quaint old Italian lady way of smacking me upside the head.

Aunt Chippy is eighty now, and I have to say, she is not really slowing down much. Her rage is just as artistic as it was when we were seven. And she still plays video poker into the wee hours of the morning, only nowadays it's a little easier for her, as Jimmy and I purchased her a video poker machine that she set up in my cousins Micki and Sally's old room.

Now she can pull out all the money she loses but doesn't get to scream at the casino manager if the machine isn't paying out. So I guess it's a win-lose for her. I love that lady and all her addictions. Smoking, yelling, and most important gambling. And if I have to show my tiny penis to all three of her daughters to prove it, I will.

BET THE HOUSE

Gambling is a lot more fun for me if the stakes are through the roof. Specifically, my roof. Multiple times in my life, and much to the chagrin of my family, I put our house on the line in a sporting event. It's not as bad as it sounds. Well, you decide.

March Madness is one of the greatest times of the year for a sports gambler. It's the perfect bridge between the end of football season and the NBA playoffs. The perennial favorites—schools like Gonzaga (which my cousin Jimmy did a pretty good job proving doesn't actually exist) and Duke (which most of the country wishes didn't exist)—competing with the Cinderella teams makes for a very entertaining and oftentimes expensive three weeks.

According to the American Gaming Association, 47 million Americans bet nearly $8.5 billion on the NCAA tournament and, miraculously enough, my degenerate friends and I are only responsible for one-third of that figure. Every March the NCAA tournament is said to cost businesses $13 billion in productivity. I guess this assumes that people aren't checking

Facebook and Instagram all day anyway. But you get the point: the NCAA tournament is a huge deal.

And it all starts with filling out a bracket. The physical act of filling out a bracket is fairly painless. I ran the office pool at *Jimmy Kimmel Live!* for fifteen years. I tried to involve everyone from the die-hard hoops fans to the people who didn't want to be bothered. I recruited anyone I could—mostly because it was funny for Jimmy to report during the monologue that, going into Final Four weekend, the woman in accounting who refused to keep a television in her house was beating seventy-five ESPN addicts.

The point is, with just a little guidance, even people who didn't know a basketball from a boccie ball were able to get through the grid. Filling out a bracket is simple. Filling out a perfect bracket is impossible. Not exactly impossible. You actually have a 1 in 9,223,372,036,854,775,808 chance of predicting every tournament game correctly from start to finish. That's 9.2 quintillion. To put that in perspective, this book has a better chance of outselling the Harry Potter franchise than you have of filling out a perfect bracket. These astronomically stupid odds led me to an astronomically brilliant idea.

I was going to offer up my house to anyone who was able to fill out a perfect bracket. My lawyer and agent advised against it—especially when I told them I was going to pull a blackjack move and pass on buying the insurance. I brought the notion to Jimmy, who thought it was a great idea, and that's all I really needed to get the wheels in motion. I went home one night after work and realized my wife also lived in that house, so I would need to convince her that I wanted to risk putting our family on the street.

I should explain that I am not good at breaking big news, specifically the timing part of breaking big news. Back in the late nineties I told my then girlfriend of eight years I was moving from New York to Los Angeles a week and a half before I left. Actually, my cousin Sally told her before I "had a chance to." Clearly payback for the exposed-penis incident. The point is, when it comes to this stuff, I am a thoughtless asshole. So when it came to telling my wife about this contest idea, I thought it best to break it to her during the car ride over to dinner…on Valentine's Day.

What better way to celebrate the love of your life than by explaining that the home we had worked decades to afford a down payment on could potentially be transferred to a stranger who spent thirty seconds scribbling down a few school names?

Well, it worked like a charm. My wife actually began weeping. When she recovered emotionally, she agreed to the contest…sort of. She announced she was never leaving the house, so she would just live with whoever won. I pictured in my mind my children being raised by the scumbag Russian hacker who was able to create an algorithm to beat my gimmick.

I checked in with other family members. When I told my mother, she disgustedly shook her head. When I told my aunt Chippy, she smacked me again.

After the concussion I suffered at her nicotine-stained hands subsided, I decided to sit down and do the math. I figured out that if things went awry and there was a perfect bracket still alive going into the final week, I would fly my fat ass out to Vegas and keep betting the results the perfect bracket had. For a few thousand dollars I could hedge my way back to the market value of my abode. That's how crazy these odds were. If there were multiple perfect brackets still in play, I'd be screwed.

The contest would run on Foxsports.com and SI.com concurrently, and Tostitos would sponsor it. We started with 250,000 entries. I requested a full report from the Web engineer after every four games as to how many people remained. By the end of Thursday night there were 15,000 left, and after Friday night there was exactly one perfect bracket remaining. That lone survivor would have to pick the next thirty-five games correctly. Not happening. In fact, the dude was eliminated after the first game on Saturday.

And here's the sick part: I was actually bummed. This wasn't nearly enough of a thrill for me. What kind of masochistic feeling was this? Kind of like asking for your broken finger to be amputated when all it needs is a splint.

Warren Buffett, one of the wisest financial minds out there, promises $1 million a year for life for the perfect bracket. But he can afford it. I own one house. Warren Buffett owns Nebraska. Yet even *he* knows not to go overboard with this gimmick.

I've already toyed with adjustments for future contests. Maybe have a perfect bracket through two weekends? Perfect through first three rounds? Eventually, I'll hand my house over on a silver platter. Pick the play-in games right and you get to live in the garage. It's just a matter of time before I lose this bet and Oleg is having his way with my wife once a week in the master bedroom.

A WRESTLING MATCH MADE IN HEAVEN

When I was thirteen years old, I ran a professional wrestling pool. Each month I'd convince a bunch of eighth-grade boys to put up $2. I always had a few extra bucks from my paper route, but almost everyone else in the pool was on a tight budget and would either skip lunch once a week or scrounge up leftover bar mitzvah loot. Some guys would pay me fifty cents a week until their $2 was paid. And in many cases, if they wanted to enter twice, they would skip up to two lunches a week. Yes, I'll admit I'm solely responsible for starting the eating disorder craze in Elwood, New York, in the mid-1980s.

Here's how it worked. I would list the top four most important matches from each of the biggest WWF cards in the area, which were typically in Madison Square Garden, Nassau Coliseum, and the Meadowlands in New Jersey. The players would pick who would emerge victorious from about twelve matches. The winner would typically have to go at least eleven out of twelve or sometimes fill out a perfect card.

The tiebreaker was the method of victory in whichever match I deemed the wild card match. So if you had a perfect slate and picked Sgt. Slaughter to defeat Mr. Fuji via cobra clutch submission and he instead won by disqualification after the referee caught Fuji throwing salt in Slaughter's eyes, you were out of luck—if someone else with a perfect card had Slaughter by DQ. I know the ladies are already getting very excited by this chapter, so I'll proceed.

Anyway, it was very heady stuff for a thirteen-year-old to keep track of. The funniest part is I did this for about two years and don't think I ever won my own pool. At the end of the month I would hand one of my buddies a fistful of quarters, which would then be deposited into a Space Invaders machine at Adventureland.

Nowadays you can still bet on wrestling through illegal offshore books, which seems insane but is actually a thing. They don't let you get rich off these anyway. Some of the online sportsbooks cap it at $50 per bet and don't allow you to make a parlay. Either way, the WWE does a nice job mixing in favorites and underdogs winning so that no one can crush the market.

Wrestling was a big part of my life in the early to mid-eighties. I idolized Rowdy Roddy Piper. Roddy was the greatest heel of all time...period. He wore a kilt to spice up his Scottish gimmick—in real life he was from Saskatoon, Canada—and was a master with the microphone. He hosted a weekly segment called *Piper's Pit* where he'd berate all the good guys or "baby faces," as they're known in the business. I remember the Saturday morning when Roddy smashed Jimmy "Superfly" Snuka in the head with a coconut. It remains the single greatest moment I've ever witnessed on free TV. Sorry, OJ.

It was a weird infatuation—even I knew it at the time—but like Roddy, I enjoyed the fact that loving the bad guy pissed people off. Especially my younger sister Ivy. She was in love with Cyndi Lauper, who somehow, through the whim of the entertainment gods, became mortal enemies with Roddy Piper. It was a perverse thrill to see Roddy kick her across the Madison Square Garden ring. My parents probably should've sent me to military school at that very moment.

Some relatives were kind enough to feed my infatuation. My aunt Joan made me a kilt that I would wear to the matches at Nassau Coliseum. Sections and sections of people would boo me. I couldn't get enough of it.

At school I would make fun of my teachers in Roddy's voice. "Look at you over there, Mr. Roth. You think you're so cool with the plaid jacket and the big blotches on your face. You'll probably give me detention for this, but I don't care. This is how I roll, brother!" One semester my Roddy impersonation was responsible for my receiving an "Uncooperative in class" comment from every one of my teachers. Every single one of them.

My father got hold of the progress report. I heard him discussing it with my mother in the kitchen. "Look at this. You know what this is? This is that Rowdy Roddy Piper bullshit." About three days later the kilt Aunt Joan made for me mysteriously disappeared.

I was all in on pro wrestling until the late eighties, and then suddenly I was turned off by how popular it became. Sort of like when people claimed they were fans of Pearl Jam when they were playing in Eddie Vedder's uncle's basement, but by their third album and millions of album sales later they had moved on to Tupac.

So that was it for me and WWE (WWF at the time) until my cousin Jimmy, maker of all dreams, surprised me at my thirtieth birthday party by flying Rowdy Roddy out for the event. Like a child's birthday gathering, Roddy came around the corner dressed to the kilt, yelling his catchphrase "I came here to kick ass and chew bubble gum...and I'm all out of bubble gum." It was an incredible entrance. Roddy stuck around for about twenty minutes telling stories. He pretended to put me in the sleeper hold. Relatives gathered and snapped pictures as if we were the Beatles. And then...he was gone. It was over-whelming. I remember being relieved that it was over. I felt like I was going to lose my shit in front of my friends and relatives.

About five years later I was at a party when my friend Kristin, who worked for WWE, suggested they start a story line for me. Kristin is great. She has a million ideas a day and I was excited because I was there to witness her only good one.

Kristin—or "KP," as her friends call her—was one of the celebrity guest bookers on *Jimmy Kimmel Live!* during its inaugural year. It didn't work out. The writing was on the wall after KP tried to book Evan Marriott (aka "Joe Millionaire") for a second time within a month. Truth be told, she once attempted to book Rodney Dangerfield three months after he passed away. Anyway, thank God she left the show, because if she didn't move on to WWE, I never would've had my magical WWE moment.

I told KP I would go along with this story line and subsequent match only if Roddy Piper "trained" me. She ran it up the flagpole and it was approved by Vince McMahon. My cousin Jimmy would have to be involved, too, of course.

My match was set to be against Santino Marella. Santino was a solid mid-card wrestler who was even better on the mic. He was a classic heel who knew how to infuriate the crowd. It was weird that I was to be the babyface in the match trained by the greatest heel of all time, but at that point it didn't matter to me. I was in the game.

We started to "build heat" by shooting a skit inside a Hooters. Santino was to interrupt my "birthday party." He and Roddy would have words and then they'd proceed to slap the shit out of each other. Really hard. Wrestling isn't as fake as people think it is.

A week later I went to Kansas City, where Santino was waiting for me in the ring with a cake that read "I'M SORRY." We were set to do a six-minute promo that would basically amount to taunting each other in a scripted exchange ending in violence. I give these guys a lot of credit: they get beat about the head in a match and then have to memorize ten-minute promos—or, worse yet, improvise.

The idea was that I was to apologize for the Hooters incident or the cake was going to end up in my face. Well, you're not going to believe this, but out of nowhere my hero Roddy Piper appeared and the cake ended up in Santino's face. That set the stage for the match at the Staples Center a few weeks later.

I trained hard for it. More than any of my one hundred or so "real" high school wrestling matches combined. I didn't want to fuck up. My assigned matchmaker-agent, Arn Anderson, one of the famed Four Horsemen of the early nineties, wrote the match out for me and I had it memorized...move for move, 1 through

45. The semipros I worked out with were great. They taught me the ropes—literally. I was too short for the top rope and my armpits and neck were getting smashed as I ran from side to side, so there were tricks to keep me from strangling myself.

In an effort to "build more heat," we shot a vignette at a boxing gym in Hollywood. Jimmy and Roddy were working me out. This time, unlike at my birthday party, Roddy choked me out for real. The sleeper hold, Roddy's patented finisher, is a very effective maneuver in real life. It's the rear naked choke hold that these days you're used to seeing in UFC matches. It's basically what the crooked cop in *Do the Right Thing* used to kill Radio Raheem minus the police baton. It does actual damage—temporarily cutting off oxygen to the brain, basically giving the recipient a mini-stroke. Roddy wasn't letting me get through his training regimen without going through some real-life shit. The funny thing is almost all of the finishing moves in pro-wrestling are, let's say, ineffective. In real life, John Cena's five-knuckle shuffle is laughable. At most, one of the knuckles connects with the side of a cheekbone on his way down. But I, of course, had to go idolize the one wrestler with a finisher that can incapacitate you. I was fortunate to survive the sleeper hold, and so it was on to the match.

19,000 fans were there, and a few of them weren't even related to me. My wife and sister with their inspirational signs sat in the front row with my buddy Dicky Barrett of the Squirrel Nut Zippers. My pals Harry and Ken showed up in Santino T-shirts. Jimmy and Roddy were in my corner. It was a lot to process. I wasn't as nervous as I thought I'd be. Santino was great in the pre-match meeting. I felt comfortable in my John Glenn High School wrestling warm-ups. It was go time!

I kept reviewing the match in my head. Fake handshake, forward roll out of the bottom position, and a headlock that transitioned into a punch to the noggin. All done. Now the hard stuff. I pulled off the airplane spin without vomiting and then the big one: a textbook suplex, which got a pop from the 19,000-plus fans at Staples.

And now for the finale. An angry Santino was expected to body-slam me, but as he bounced off the ropes, he would get tripped up by my cousin Jimmy, and I would place a stunned Santino in a cradle for the win.

Only problem is Jimmy got caught watching the match and forgot his part in the finish. Santino wisely stopped to argue with Jimmy, so it was up to me to improvise an ending. It wasn't too difficult: I had seen it done 1,000 times before. I came up from behind and rolled Santino up for the pin. 1... 2...3...*I win!* This match lives online and I can guarantee you I am solely responsible for 86,955 of the 87,000 YouTube views. If you're interested, a quick search of "Sal and Santino" will get you there.

Aside from, and including, the birth of my children, this was the single greatest thrill of my half century on earth. I only hope that somewhere a lunatic thirteen-year-old boy bet on my match and was able to take home forty bucks in quarters.

In the years to follow, I became very close with Roddy Piper. He wanted to get into comedy and I helped him develop a one-man show. He started to get respect as a comedian at places like the Comedy Store. Why wouldn't he? He was one of the funniest storytellers anyone knew.

Roddy and I had countless dinners at the Hollywood Roosevelt Hotel, where he'd regale me and my friend Jake with crazy stories about his life. My wife made him his favorite dish, shepherd's pie, as we watched a screener of *The Wrestler* in my living room. I put him in our Christmas card one year. So many great memories with Roddy, who couldn't have been more of a teddy bear in real life.

Roddy always referred to me as "my pal Sal." Here's how a routine conversation would go. He'd call me on the phone...

Roddy: My pal Sal, where are your kids right now?
Me: They're in the yard playing baseball.
Roddy: Why aren't you with them?
Me: I'm talking to you, my pal. [I liked to return the favor.]
Roddy: I want you to hang up the phone right now and kiss them all on the head and tell them how proud of them you are.

Choked up, but not wanting to get choked out, I'd do it every time. He was a true gentleman who taught me a lot about how to be a caring father.

I am writing this chapter on the fifth anniversary of his passing. His death came as a shock to me. I realize none of us are invincible, but when the toughest guy you know ceases to exist, it shakes you to the core.

I miss Roddy Piper dearly and thank him for the opportunity of a lifetime and for his friendship.

And I'll continue to honor him until long after I'm all out of bubble gum.

SHOTGUN!

By the end of high school my sports gambling career was in full swing. They say it's not what you know, it's who you know, and—lucky for me (luckier for him)—by eighteen years old I had become acquainted with the local bookie.

Full disclosure: that man's name is Lloyd. Fuller disclosure: that man's name is not Lloyd.

I changed his name so he isn't brought up on tax evasion charges.

I've spoken on the phone with or texted Lloyd more than anyone I've ever known...possibly combined. And I've never met the man in person. He's just a voice coming out of a box— like Charlie to my Angel—except, as far as I can remember, the Angels were never forced to pay Charlie every Monday after some dirtbag kicker from Ohio State missed a chip shot field goal as time expired.

Anyway, one Sunday morning in December of 1989, I snuck down to the basement and called Lloyd to turn in another slate of losing NFL picks, when I was interrupted by my father opening and closing the door behind me. I wasn't sure how much he had heard. I definitely didn't need him knowing that I was gambling.

My parents aren't big bettors unless you count the tremendous risk my mother took by having children with my father. This and the occasional switching of tags on clothes at Marshalls is the only real chance she would routinely take. My mother lost both her parents, her brother, and her sister at a fairly young age. She's a wonderful and giving lady—the strongest person I've ever met and forever an inspiration to me.

In addition to her amazing qualities as a human and the fact that she routinely parks at least twenty-seven inches from the curb, my mother also has a great head for math, which I'm pretty sure I inherited.

But I don't blame her. To be honest, despite what I said above, my father wasn't totally against risking money on chance. He himself had stories of taking horse racing bets as a youth from neighbors. That was a successful business until he decided not to pay out the winners.

But it was different for him, as that was a very Brooklyn thing to do in the 1960s. In fact, back then, if you were in your mid-twenties and living in Brooklyn and still didn't have a story about either stealing hubcaps, lighting a neighbor's porch ablaze from a fireworks accident, or not turning in winning bets, you were immediately shipped upstate to Poughkeepsie.

That's just the way the cannoli crumbled. But, more important, people from Brooklyn and especially of Italian American descent were all about teaching lessons. And I was about to learn a valuable one.

As soon as I made my way up the steps, my father asked

to speak with me. I knew he wasn't seeking my opinion on whether we should go with a Norfolk Island pine or Douglas fir Christmas tree this year. He called me into the garage, which I thought was very odd. My father was a man who never minded dressing me down in front of the family or the neighbors or even a door-knocking Jehovah's Witness, for that matter. The request for privacy had me baffled, but I followed him into the garage, where he proceeded to reach into a mysterious sliding cabinet.

As far as I knew, the only items in those cabinets were tools and a rifle that he kept secret but that my friends and I had known was there for years.

This was making less and less sense. I knew I had screwed up, but did betting on the Buccaneers on a private line really warrant death, execution-style? Or maybe his plan was to hacksaw my tongue off to make sure I could never phone in a losing bet again. Luckily for me, my father had more reasonable plans as he reached into the toolbox and pulled out a check that was made out to him from his boss.

My father was a salesman who peddled fragrances to military personnel, which never really made sense to me. Do servicemen care about how they smell in the trenches?

Apparently the answer was yes, as my dad was able to make a decent living of it. This particular year he had met a sales quota and received a bonus check for $3,000.

"You see this?" he said, holding up the check. "This is the only way to get ahead in life. Hard work!"

I was happy for him but confused as to why he had hidden the check by his weapons and tools. I guess just in case the bad guys came in the middle of the night to force him to endorse it over to them? Maybe he wanted to place a bet and I missed the signal.

Either way, I wasn't going to argue with him—mainly because kickoff was in ten minutes and I had to make my way to the Sporting Grill, which was the only bar in town that admitted nineteen-year-old bookies.

Bottom line: Lloyd and I were meant to be, and there was nothing that was going to get in the way of our love affair with the betting lines.

At the same time I realized my old man was right. I think subconsciously I must've known that a few years later Robert De Niro in *A Bronx Tale* would pound home the point to his son, Calogero, that the workingman was not a sucker.

In this real-life scenario my father was the workingman with a working hacksaw and a working rifle—and I was the sucker, which I guess is a good thing because otherwise there would be no book.

DON'T READ THIS STORY; IT'S GROSS

One of the great thrills of my life was the first time a betting service put odds on an event that I was featured in. My buddy Bill Simmons's childhood friend Joe House had a segment called *House Eats* that lived on Grantland.com. In these masterful videos House would celebrate all kinds of delicacies. He later parlayed this into a popular food podcast called *House of Carbs* as well as a cholesterol level so out of control Lipitor stock spiked to record highs.

House Eats 1 and *2* featured Joe stopping at a roadside diner on his way to Vegas and a Chinese restaurant in LA called Yang Chow.

The first two installments were entertaining but focused on an appreciation of food. *House Eats 3* was all about good old-fashioned carnivorous gluttony. House and I would trade protein punches in an eating competition in New Orleans.

The event would take place February 1, 2013, at the Acme

Oyster House in New Orleans. We were there for the Super Bowl between the Ravens and the 49ers. But trust me: this matchup was the real Super Bowl.

Bovada installed House as a slight –130 favorite to be the prevailing pig, which upset me beyond comprehension. These people clearly hadn't done their research. They obviously weren't clued in about the summer of '87 when I came in third out of fifty kids in a blueberry pie–eating contest at wrestling camp in Stroudsburg, Pennsylvania. This feat was especially impressive inasmuch as we were there to get in shape and lose weight.

They also obviously weren't keen on the damage I had done at various Long Island Sizzlers restaurants back in the early nineties. One particular incident led to a post-meal vomit session on the side of the road. A little boy witnessed this and ran into his house. "Mommy, a man is throwing up in our yard!"

A low point in my life for sure. Or maybe a high point, depending on how you look at it.

• • •
• • •

My crowning eating achievement came in 1992 at an establishment called Popei's. Not the popular chicken restaurant that stole the name of a spinach-eating dwarf strongman. This Popei's was a dive seafood restaurant in Kings Park, Long Island, that offered weird specials. One of them was billed the "Popei's Challenge": $39.95 for two pounds of pasta, a plate of clams and mussels, twenty chicken wings, vegetables, and a baked potato. But there was a hook. If you could finish it all in under ninety minutes, Popei's would pick up the tab.

My childhood buddies Darren, Sneaky Joe, Naabes, Lazy

Larry, and Finkin would join me to witness my quest for a free feast.

They're all lunatics in their own regard, but on this night they were focused on my lunacy. In my circle, completing the Popei's Challenge was much more of an achievement than finishing law school or having a child. This was the real deal.

We sat down. I ordered the special and waited for all shellfish hell to break loose.

I should point out that there was a fair amount of psychology involved in this Challenge from a Popei's perspective. First of all, in an attempt to overwhelm you, they present the entire meal at once. Then, one by one, the waitresses approach you and tell you how, in their 793 combined years of serving, they've never seen anyone complete the Popei's Challenge.

None of this was going to work on me. I was in a zone like mid-nineties Michael Jordan against the Knicks.

"Start the clock!" I exclaimed as they dropped the last of the monstrous plates in front of me. I had ninety minutes—no time-outs. And unlike soccer, no bullshit injury time added at the end. So if I sliced my thumb opening a clam and needed to be stitched up, that was on me.

It really was an overwhelming amount of food. My plan was to attack one item at a time. First, the twenty wings. I knew this wasn't going to present too much of a problem. I was familiar with Popei's wing sauce, and during a practice run a few weeks before, I had devoured forty-five of them.

Also, I attended college in upstate New York, where if you can't polish off three dozen wings during orientation, they don't let you matriculate.

The wings were done with. Sixty-two minutes remaining.

Time to move on to the seafood. The work of getting the slimy fish out of the shells was actually the most time-consuming element, but my buddies helped out, so it became a nonissue.

If the restaurant manager had been smart, he would have crazy-glued the mussels shut—but he didn't, and so, with forty-two minutes remaining, I had only two pounds of pasta, baked potato, and vegetables left.

I remember taking a big swig of my iced tea (to which I'd added, ironically, a packet of Sweet'N Low) and ripping right through the baked potato.

I took a short respite. Almost half the allotted time remained.

I had saved the worst for last. Two pounds of pasta and a Costco full of vegetables.

I would alternate. Forkful of vegetables. Forkful of pasta. It was at this point that I began sweating. One waitress could sense I was slowing down. "Ah, you poor thing. You're not going to do it." More head games.

At the one-hour-and-ten-minute mark I busted through half the pasta and vegetables. I was really starting to feel it. On this evening, there would be no dessert.

Waitress #2 checks in. "You gave it your best. Congratulations! You have nothing to be ashamed of."

I had plenty of things to be ashamed of, but finishing this was not one of them.

At the one-hour-and-fifteen-minute mark, I had about a quarter pound of pasta and vegetables remaining and was bursting at the seams.

Waitress #3: "We're proud of you no matter what!"

Now I'm getting pissed. I'm convinced that last one wasn't even a waitress—she was a hired all-you-can-eat-restaurant taunter. Sort of like the flunky version of William H. Macy's character in *The Cooler.*

At this point my friends—who just a few hours before were cursing me as I won the weekly mini-Sega '93 hockey tourney (my house, so I got to use the loose joystick and play the Red Wings)—were fully in my corner. They were now more into this than I was. Partly because they didn't want to pony up $36.95 to pay for their unemployed friend and partly because they knew they were witnessing greatness.

Twelve minutes left. I begin to figure it mathematically. Probably twenty-five to thirty more for forkfuls of pasta and vegetables. I was spent. It wasn't happening.

No pep talk was going to put me over. Adrian Balboa could've dragged me to the beach and given me the "What's the truth, dammit?!?!" speech and it wouldn't have helped. I was so delirious, it wasn't physically possible to hold down even three more noodles never mind a stalk of cauliflower.

What a bummer! Imagine losing a competitive-eating contest because you didn't finish your vegetables. Such a mixed message haunting you from your youth.

I may not have finished, but I'd be damned if I was paying for this mess. The fellas and I put our heads together and came up with a plan. We were going to hide the evidence.

Everyone would play a part in this petty theft. Sneaky Joe and Naabes would go hit on the waitresses to keep them distracted. (They broke the ice by bragging about coming in second and third in our Sega tournament. Women love that shit.)

Darren and Lazy Larry would be on the lookout for

suspicious-looking manager types. Finkin would sit there and not say a word: I loved him, but he had a big mouth. If he ruined this for me, I would run him over with his own Honda Del Sol.

There were six minutes left when I decided to make use of a potted plant. Yep, my resourceful instincts had kicked in. These vegetables would become one with the plant. My finest composting work ever. I was on a mission, and half my problems were solved.

Now for the leftover pasta. I had to get rid of it. There was only one option. My sneakers. My poor two-day-old Nike high-tops would have to pay the price for my stomach's shortcomings. I slipped them off, slyly shoved the leftover linguine into my shoes, and squished my feet back in.

There...done.

Darren and Finkin started the applause. Naabes and Sneaky Joe stopped chatting up the female staffers as they all came over to marvel at the spectacle.

Waitress 1: This is unbelievable!

Waitress 2: We've seen guys three times your size try and fail!

Manager: We need to take a picture.

Me: No, thanks. No picture. I need to get out of here before I throw up all over your already horrified customers.

Finkin: He's not kidding—he throws up a lot.

Darren led me out the front door as the others squared away the rest of the bill. I left triumphantly, linguini sprouting from my brand-new shoes. On the way home, I was forced to toss them out the window. I sacrificed a $75 pair of Nike high-tops for a $36.95 meal.

• • •
• • •

Sadly, Bovada wasn't privy to my legendary Popei's Challenge effort—so. Twenty-five years later, Joe House remained a favorite to dethrone me as King of the Onion Ring.

Before I go into this further, I have to warn you that *House Eats 3* was one of the grossest events I've ever witnessed, let alone facilitated. It was so disturbing that when Grantland posted the video, Bill Simmons was forced by ESPN to offer a disclaimer, basically begging people not to watch.

The event took place on the Friday before the Super Bowl. I was superconfident. In an effort to psyche House out, I wore a Kamala T-shirt. Kamala was an obese, painted-up eighties professional wrestler who claimed to be from Uganda but was actually from a poorer town in Mississippi. He was a gigantic dude who would smack his humongous belly during matches. Kamala would routinely gain twenty-five pounds per week. Later in life he lost his legs to diabetes. He was my inspiration.

The rules were as follows. Whoever could eat the most food in an hour and a half would be declared the winner. The only caveat was you had to keep everything you swallowed down for the full ninety minutes. As the aforementioned little boy who lived a block away from the Sizzler could attest, this has often been an obstacle for me.

In addition to Simmons, Grantland writer Rembert Browne and Nathan Hubbard who, at the time was CEO of Ticketmaster, would serve as judges. I liked Rembert and Nathan very much, although I question the idea that any CEO of anything would agree to participate in an event as disturbing as this.

A lady named Maria was unfortunately given the midday Friday shift and would serve as our waitress. She started the clock and immediately dropped the first two courses: Louisiana oysters and steamed crawfish. Protein. Easy. House and I polished off our plates without blinking.

Then came blue fries with roast beef gravy and chicken seafood gumbo. Which, by the way, is spectacular. Whoever came up with this combination should probably receive both a Nobel Prize and the electric chair.

Then red beans and rice and chicken étouffée. They were throwing the kitchen sink at us and it was bouncing right back off my belly. House, on the other hand, was slow-playing it. After the twelve-minute mark all three judges had me ahead.

I was feeling good about this. House was a connoisseur of food who dabbled in overeating. I was a consumption cannibal. He sensed that he was out of his league. At least, I thought this was the case.

Out came the "10 Napkin Roast Beef" plate. Now it's starting to get ridiculous. Nothing that doesn't occur in the privacy of your bedroom when your wife is away should require ten napkins.

Speaking of filthy references, it was at this point that House requested a bathroom break but asked if someone would monitor him to make sure nothing weird was going on, I guess insinuating that he might pleasure himself after consuming 4,500 calories? Now I was worried.

Jambalaya, shrimp étouffée, soft-shell crab...followed by the thirteenth course: fish Te'o. House and I crushed them all.

House was making a comeback, but was still behind. We decided collectively to take a bathroom break to throw water on our faces. Things didn't work out as planned for me. Two steps into the restroom and there it was. I vomited all over the floor. A fire hydrant of fried fish.

House ran out pumping his fists in celebration. He did everything but rip off his sports bra.

According to the rules he was already declared the winner...UNLESS I was able to use the remaining time to replenish my gut and overtake his caloric consumption.

To my credit, I did try to get back in the game. I walked back from the restroom and received an ovation. The crowd admired the fact that I was continuing. I was praying for a Willis Reed game 7 moment.

I grabbed what I could and stuffed my fat face with whatever remained of the first thirteen courses. House, on the other hand, quit eating with ten minutes remaining. The bayou was beginning to affect his bowels.

I kept going with the desserts: ice cream bread pudding and bananas Foster cheesecake. But it was all in vain. I couldn't make up the difference. My only hope was to make House spill his guts. I could see he was in rough shape, so I leaped from my seat and tried to get behind him to squeeze his stomach.

If I could pull the Heimlich maneuver on a bloated guy, I might have a chance. But House knew what I was up to and as the horrified crowd counted down from 20, I decided to chase House around the table. It was Benny Hill meets Ben & Jerry's meets Benihana.

Try as I might, I couldn't catch him, and so the result would have to stick. Now all we had to do was hear from the judges.

Rembert and Nathan were appreciative of my effort but declared House the winner. Simmons's vote no longer mattered, but I was going to make him pay for it either way. Forget Willis Reed: this was my Lardass moment in *Stand by Me*. But instead of castor oil, I was using my own finger. As Simmons went through his analysis, I stuck a digit down my throat. The plan was to let it go all over his lap, but Simmons knew what I was trying to do and quickly scurried out of the way. I honestly believe if I had my way and puked on him that we wouldn't be friends right now.

Instead, I projectile vomited on a table of leftover food. Multiple times. In between the three extra rounds of heaving, I commented that we might have to tip Maria three or four more dollars.

As I dejectedly wiped crawfish upchuck from my mouth, I was able to muster one more important decree: "I'm taking the 49ers −3."

Fittingly, a losing Super Bowl pick. Add crow to the list of things I ate that day.

WORST CHOICES AT A VEGAS BUFFET

CUSTOMER RECEIPT

Mashed potatoes (cheap and fills you up) (5/2)

Pickled squid (4/1)

Chickpeas (9/2)

Anything previously breathed on by a stripper (7/1)

Win total:

Total bet:

65988 - 4 4807802443545 379045345- 3 678 4534 3 -4 678 678353 678534

STONE COLD SCAM

If you were involved in illegal sports gambling in the mid-nineties, there's an excellent chance you were unfortunate enough to land on a handicapper dummy list. This somewhat elite group of degenerates was targeted by people pretending to have inside information on games. "Team A got food poisoning from eating bad clam chowder on the bus" was one of my favorite fabricated tales.

In reality, these lowlifes knew nothing more than the average fan. In most cases, less. They are complete scum. Like if meter maids mated with Nigerian prince scammers, except one hundred times as relentless and uncaring.

I was getting good at hanging up on these clowns.

"Hello, Sal, this is Bob Banks. Are you ready to make some money?"

"Sorry, Bob, can't talk now, I'm on my way out to eat."

"Well, are you eating lobster tonight? Because if you listen to me you could—" CLICK.

You couldn't let them speak; otherwise they would eventually draw you into their web of degenerate deceit. Their entire spiel was fake, starting with their made-up names, which all contained one syllable and had some connection to gambling or winning money. Bob Banks, Bruce Locke, Dale Cash...they all had my number and I had theirs.

And then there was Mike Stone. This guy spotted a sucker in my friend Harry a mile away.

Have I not told you about Harry yet? Buckle in. Harry was my best friend in college. I met him freshman year at Oswego State University. He was what other students called a "townie," having been raised within the city limits. This is a big deal in Oswego, as the city boasts not only the most bars per square mile but also a gorgeous nuclear power plant right smack in the middle of the city. This, in addition to his bald head and abnormally directed eyes made Harry a real-life Homer Simpson, prompting his fraternity brothers to nickname him "Homer."

But appearance was the least of Harry's worries. Maybe second least. Harry was addicted to games of chance. He didn't have a gambling bug, he had a gambling infestation. So much so that after college, on his way to taking a job at CNN in Georgia, Harry kept heading west—straight to the desert, settling down in Sin City.

Harry had majored in broadcasting and even set himself up with a $700 toupee in the hopes of becoming the next Fred Hickman, an obscure cable sports reporter from the eighties. (Don't you dare feel bad about not knowing who I'm referring to.)

But gambling was Harry's true love, so that was the CN-end for journalism. The whole thing was actually my fault. A few months before this baffling decision, some of my high school friends—Darren, Joey, Naabes, and Finkin—decided we would ditch our families and spend Christmas with my aunt Joan and uncle Jimmy in Phoenix and then New Years in Las Vegas with my aunt Chippy and uncle Frank. I'm not even sure they invited us. I am sure that we invited Harry, who couldn't be happier to say yes. Of course, while in Vegas, we gambled like lunatics. Naabes lost all his money immediately...like before we even retrieved our bags from the luggage carousel.

The rest of us lost our money gradually—except for Harry, who won a lot playing roulette. He was hitting everything. He had a weird knack of stacking chips around certain numbers. He claims he was able to read the dealer's roll. When the roulette ball would bounce into his number, he would rejoice. When it bounced out of his number and into another, he would blame the wheel. But all in all it was a very profitable week for Harry, who took home around $7,000—enough to purchase all of Oswego, New York.

Buoyed by his mastery of the wheel, a few months later, Harry ditched the CNN job and returned to Las Vegas, this time with the intention of becoming a full-time Las Vegan. Roulette would now be his occupation. He figured he had a system. And he was right. Only problem was the casinos had a system, too. In a matter of a week Harry went on to lose everything. He became roulette illiterate. He could no longer "read the roll."

He had a roulette system malfunction. In college he didn't have a functioning sports gambling system, either, which is why the Mike Stones of the world were able to pick away at Harry's confused carcass.

To Harry's credit, this particular scam artist had given him three free winners in as many days before he requested $400 for future picks. That's when Mike Stone dangled his "Stone-cold lock of the year" and Harry bought it hook, line, and stinker.

The guaranteed winner was going to be revealed a few minutes before kickoff on Saturday.

This was another clever way for the scumbag handicappers to build drama while inflicting more psychological damage on their victims. Harry was only too happy to part with the money he had made over the summer working at the local nuclear power plant. (His previous line of work goes a long way toward explaining Harry's physical appearance, as you'll see in the photo insert.)

He sent $400 to Stone via Western Union and waited until an hour before kickoff on Saturday before receiving the pick.

It's important to note that Mike Stone wasn't taking the bet. He was just accepting money for the pick. In order to earn a profit, Harry had to cover the money he paid Stone with his wager, so he took out seven hundred additional dollars and bet Stone's pick, Western Michigan +37.5, through his local bookie.

Now, you have to remember, this was a lot of loot for Harry back then. To put this into perspective, thirty years later Harry still struggles to earn $700 a week. And I'm including the money he received in his settlement with a local resort in Phoenix where a Sri Lankan bathroom attendant allegedly grabbed his junk. But that's a story for another book.

You also have to remember that Florida State was a powerhouse in the early to mid-nineties. Bobby Bowden's team saw six players drafted from that '91 squad, including quarterbacks Brad Johnson and Casey Weldon, running backs Edgar Bennett and Amp Lee, and defensive back Terrell Buckley.

Western Michigan, on the other hand, didn't have six players drafted during the entire twentieth century. Don't bother looking it up. It's one of those exaggerations that's likely 100 percent accurate.

But 37.5 is a lot of points, and if Mike Stone was willing to stake his pristine reputation on the lowly Broncos, then Harry figured it was worth a shot.

I don't even have to tell you how this ended, but I will anyway. Final score: Florida State 58, Western Michigan 0.

The game wasn't televised, so Harry got updates every thirty minutes on the ESPN scroll. It was still painful, and Harry figured he'd get his money's worth the next day by calling Stone to give him a piece of his feeble mind.

Harry: Let me ask you something, Mike. What kind of fucking idiot gives out a team that doesn't score as his lock of the year?

Mike Stone: Let me ask YOU something, Harry. What kind of fucking idiot gives $400 to a perfect stranger? [CLICK]

In retrospect, Mike's was the better of the questions. I honestly don't think Harry ever recovered from that moment. And it was made worse a few years later when we learned how these scam artists operated.

First, they'd get hold of a list of about two hundred idiots like Harry. Let's say the Oilers were playing the Steelers on a

Sunday. They'd tell one hundred people the Oilers were going to cover and tell the other one hundred that the Steelers were going to cover. Then on Monday they'd call the one hundred people they gave the winner to and tell fifty of them the Rockets would cover against the Trailblazer and the other fifty would get the opposite side. Now they've given out two winners to fifty people.

Eventually they'd split the list, so that by Wednesday a dozen degenerates would have four winners.

At this point you'd believe they knew what they were talking about, and that's when they pounced.

This is tougher to pull off in the age of the Internet, but there will always be a Mike Stone as long as the Harrys of the world are legally allowed online.

In the meantime, I put "What kind of fucking idiot gives $400 to a perfect stranger?" up there among the great existential questions of all time.

RIGGED GIG

My first real wake-up call gambling-wise came in the spring of 1991. I was a sophomore in college and was on a terrible losing streak and was just trying to stay above water until the NCAA tournament. That's when all the fun starts. This year, though, the fun wasn't meant to be. South Alabama played Old Dominion in the Sun Belt Championship—a game that both teams needed to win to get into the NCAA tournament. The game somehow aired on ESPN.

This was that weird no-man's-land on ESPN, post–Australian Rules Football but before Disney wrangled NBA rights for the worldwide leader.

Anyway, my last resort bet was South Alabama laying 7 points. I knew nothing about this team. Didn't know the coach. Didn't know any of the players. I wasn't even sure what state South Alabama was in. I'm guessing Mississippi.

All I knew was they had beaten their previous Sun Belt foes by 26 and 27 points. Good enough intel for me.

Well, you know how this goes. South Alabama was up 5

with about twenty seconds left...They heaved a 3-pointer that just missed and won the game by 5.

No cover. I lost again. Only this time I didn't have money to pay my debt. The job market wasn't exactly booming in Oswego, New York, in the early 1990s. My only real opportunity to earn was to work at the campus dining hall, but I had cruel, idiot friends who threatened to toss tater tots at my head if I was behind the counter, so that wasn't happening.

Like an angel from the handicapping heavens, my bookie Hotter stepped up. Hotter was somehow in charge of running the local rec league. He gave Harry and me gigs refereeing the seventh-grade basketball games after school. We would be paid $6 each per game, which meant I would be done paying off my debt when the children reached thirty-seventh grade.

A steep hill to climb, but a nice gesture by Hotter, nonetheless. Certainly more civil than sending some goon from the rugby team to bust up our thumbs. We really had no choice, so we made the best of it.

I didn't have much practical experience refereeing basketball games—unless you count watching the hundreds of games I had bet on and lost on television—but I started to get the hang of it and at the same time enjoyed it. I found that there was nothing more gratifying than fouling some punk kid out of a game and watching him and his white-trash girlfriend walk out cursing you at the top of his lungs. The berating brought me back to the days when I used to wear a kilt at Nassau Coliseum in support of Rowdy Roddy Piper.

But eventually refereeing became boring for me and Harry, and when you're bored, you do dumb things, like start betting on the games you're refereeing.

We were making $6 per game but betting each other $10 on that same game. Harry would wager on one team and I would take the other. This preceded NBA referee Tim Donaghy's malfeasance by a few years, so we didn't have anyone to look up to in this regard.

At first we were cool about it. Maybe we'd call a block when it was 75 percent a charge; or if the ball kicked out of bounds off a player's shin, Harry would call it off the kid who was guarding him. We really should've gotten college credit for an acting class, because explaining why we were making these calls to the middle school kids was a skill that we honed pretty well.

As the stakes got higher, the calls got worse. Phantom travels, three-second violations, technical fouls for kids who cursed themselves after a missed free throw. It was all fair game. Harry and I were reenacting Leslie Nielsen's umpire role in *The Naked Gun* and everyone started to notice. Over the course of a few weeks I almost got jumped by a half a dozen twelve-year-olds, their fathers, and their grandmothers. Eventually someone lodged a complaint, the news got back to Hotter, and we were ousted as referees. True to his name, Hotter was hot when he got ahold of us. He lectured me and Harry on integrity, which seemed hilarious coming from a local bookie running a rec league. At some point he even sarcastically threw in that Harry and I didn't deserve jobs mopping up at a Waffle House in South Alabama. Even a shitty referee like me could tell that was an offensive foul, but word to the wise: it's better to get into business with a bookie who prefers breaking spirits to breaking thumbs.

LET'S MUCK A DEAL

When I was young, I was infatuated with how people earned their money. It made sense to me that doctors and baseball players made a good living, but immense wealth didn't add up to me for two specific occupations.

One was the attendant who paraded around holding a wad of cash at the local full-service gas station. It took a while for me to figure out that the twenty-something-year-old stoner didn't get to keep the loot. He needed to flaunt the hunk of bills to make change just long enough until some asshole robbed him and took off down Jericho Turnpike.

The other was the potbellied bearded man who was able to rake in tens of thousands of dollars playing poker without moving from his seat. I remember watching the World Series of Poker as a kid on ESPN. Sweathog wrangler Gabe Kaplan would do the play-by-play for the events. It was different from the way they do it now, because back then YOU COULDN'T SEE THE

HOLD CARDS. That's right: nowadays there's a camera that catches the cards when they're raked in. The other players can't see, but those following at home can. But back in the early to mid-eighties no one could see shit.

> **Kaplan:** I'm looking at Amarillo Slim's face here…He could have king/10 suited…maybe ace/5 unsuited. It's hard to tell.

No, Gabe, it's actually impossible to tell. Mr. Kotter had an easier time teaching Horshack and Barbarino about photosynthesis than he did speculating for early-eighties ESPN viewers on what cards were facedown.

Part of the problem was that the players didn't trust any cameras on the table. You can't blame them for not wanting extra technology that could lend itself to cheating. Especially since we were only a couple of decades removed from Texas Hold 'Em tournaments regularly being settled with gunfire.

But eventually the players realized it was better for the game's popularity to have the audience be able to follow what the hell was going on. And let me say this: the guy who invented the pocket card cam, along with the dude who finally decided it was time to put wheels on luggage, deserves a Nobel Prize. Or Noble Prize, depending on how the president of your home nation calls it.

Presenting poker in a watchable format allowed viewers to familiarize themselves with some of the game's more offbeat personalities.

Phil Hellmuth is my favorite. He's nicknamed "the Brat," and for good reason. If anyone beats him he claims it was complete luck and makes his opponent feel like an asshole for bluffing or betting or whatever they did to beat him. Never once has he said, "Ah, you got me."

It's kind of how I lead my gambling life. I can win ten consecutive basketball bets in overtime, and if the ref makes a bad call to cost me the eleventh game, I lose my mind. It's an endearing quality for sure and definitely makes people want to be around you a lot.

The other thing that Hellmuth does is he shows up late. This is not how I like to live my life. I'm always early to things, but Hellmuth does it as a power play. He likes to make a grand entrance, sometimes hours into a card game. Of course, the dealer will collect his ante every time the button comes around to his empty seat, but it's worth the automatic losses to see what it does to the other players' psyches.

He's also really fucking good. Hellmuth has more bracelets than Don Rickles's wife.

And while he was one of the top players, poker didn't really get that burst until 2003 when a man named Chris Moneymaker won the main event bracelet and $2.5 million.

In doing so, Moneymaker became the first winner to qualify from an online poker event. The new surge in popularity became referred to as "the Moneymaker Effect."

Before then, in order to get into the main event, the players had to either get sponsored, win a live tournament, or pay a $10,000 entry fee. Getting a free pass from an online tournament opened things up for the game in a big way. Now anyone with a credit card, Wi-Fi, and a respectable gambling problem can gain entrance into the World Series of Poker without ever leaving his grandmother's basement.

Moneymaker was the poster boy for underdog card players everywhere. He was chubby and sloppy, which gave everyone—especially me—hope.

I never really had the poker bug. My first agent used to have poker night at his house. That almost always ended in an argument and a bunch of IOUs. I played a little online. I'd win. I'd lose. On a good night, maybe after a couple hours, I'd place third in a twenty-player tournament and clear fifty bucks. I certainly wasn't making a living off of it. Also, I didn't trust it. I was always suspicious about seven degenerate friends teaming up and cleaning out two poor schlubs who unfortunately ended up in the same room as them. History proved me right, and, as a result, most of these sites have been shut down.

But none of that made a difference to me when, the year after Moneymaker won, Harrah's Hotel approached me and offered to stake my run if *Jimmy Kimmel Live!* would document it. My cousin Jimmy gave the okay, and the next thing I knew, we were sent with a camera crew to the Rio hotel, setting up for anywhere from a six-minute to a six-day run.

I had befriended poker pro Chris Ferguson (ninety-plus World Series of Poker wins totaling more than $6 million in earnings) in the days leading up to the event. Ferguson was nicknamed Jesus—I'm guessing because he was a ruthless bluffer, but also probably more for his trademark long hair and beard. Jesus taught me some tricks and a basic strategy but I wasn't really taking it seriously.

I expected an early exit. In fact, we had Southwest flights booked for that same evening but never made our way onto that plane, as I somehow ended up lasting until the third day of competition. To be fair, if you survived the first day, you got the second day off—so I just spent that free time drinking nonalcoholic piña coladas (I'm an old Mormon woman when it comes to booze) by the Rio pool. But that first day was a miracle.

As I said, my goal was to come away from this with a comedy bit. I was going to attempt to unnerve the other players by singing stupid songs, flossing my teeth, laughing for no reason, etc. Instead I somehow became a legitimate threat. All afternoon I was dealt pairs of face cards, ended with straights off the flop, and got lucky with flushes on the river card. There was barely any skill involved; I was just running hot. After the first day I was in the top 10 percent.

By the third day I started to become a decent-sized Vegas story. Not huge, but somewhere in between Tupac's shooting and a new deli opening up in Henderson. Unfortunately, when you get notoriety, people start playing more aggressively, trying to knock you out. By the evening of the third night I had about $18,000 in chips, which seems like a lot but was still vulnerable to attack from bigger sharks.

During one of the breaks I got on the phone with Jesus, who offered me some advice. "You're playing too tight. You can't be afraid to lose."

I took that advice—went all in on the first hand out of the break and busted just an hour outside of making it to the money round. Thanks for nothing, Jesus.

I was actually relieved but looked over at the producer, Jen, and the director, Brad, and they looked at me as if they were about to burst into tears. I reminded them that this was a positive in that we finally were able to go to our homes, and so we did.

After that, I distanced myself from the poker craze. It

would've been bad for me. With the ease at which you could play online anytime you were bored, I absolutely would've lost everything I had.

I still like playing in Vegas once in a while late at night when I can't sleep. Recently I sat down to a 2/4 no-limit game at the Bellagio. After a couple hours of almost no action, I decided to play a decent hand: a pair of queens. I went head-to-head with a fellow who looked like a really old, weathered version of Sting. Every breath he took could have been his last, but he was hanging around the hand, and after an insignificant flop and turn card we both checked.

The dealer's river was a five of hearts. Didn't help me, but, win or lose, this was my last hand of the evening. So if he bet, I'd match him just to see his card.

And then...the stare down. Old Man Sting locked eyes with me. My hidden camera bit training had taught me how to act very cool in ridiculous situations, so this should have been easy. Only problem was it was close to 4:00 a.m. now so my eyes were watering up. I was blinking like a firefly on Molly, so I imagine my tells were all over the place.

At that point we were entering minute 3 of the stare down, which seemed like an eternity. I didn't understand the torture. The King of Pain doppelgänger was really making me suffer. Why couldn't this guy just bet so we could call it a night. At the five-minute mark I had had enough.

Me: You gonna bet anytime tonight or are we just going to stare at each other until breakfast?
Old Man Sting: It's your turn to bet, dude.
Me: Oh, sorry...check.

Old Man Sting: Check.

Dealer flipped over a deuce on the river. Old Man Sting turned over a pair of kings. I lost. Good night.

Moral of the story: Always choose sleep over queens.

THE MIGHTY KASAY STRIKES OUT

It's not often that you get a chance to affect the outcome of a game you bet on. As far as I know, I am one of the few civilians who have actually used my evil powers to influence the final score of a game viewed by over 140 million people. That's right: I singlehandedly changed the result of Super Bowl XXXVIII. At least, that's how it went down in my mind.

It was 2004 when the Patriots—not nearly as ruthless and despicable as they are now—were facing the Carolina Panthers in the NFL championship game. (That's how we're supposed to say it if we don't want to spend the rest of our lives on Riker's Island.) My cousin's late-night talk show, *Jimmy Kimmel Live!*, was establishing itself as the gold standard in pranks, and when it came to creating mischief, I was their guy.

We wanted to do something that would make a splash, so

we targeted Media Day. For those of you unfamiliar, Media Day is an event that was held (at the time) on the Tuesday before the Super Bowl. It gives the press an opportunity to ask hard-hitting questions such as "Can you believe you're here?" and "What motivates you?"

No one ever learns a thing about the players at Media Day. For the most part they are stoic and robotic and the best part is the whole time they're doling out these nothing answers, they are wearing their uniforms. It's like the world's most sober costume party.

My cousin Jimmy and I decided that I would attend Media Day dressed up like one of the players.

My choices were Panthers placekicker John Kasay or wide receiver Muhsin Muhammad.

Actually, my only choice was John Kasay. That was it, really. I could only pass for a kicker, and the Patriots' Adam Vinatieri had already become world-famous after booting the game-winning field goal against the Rams a couple Super Bowls earlier, so Kasay was my guy.

John Kasay was listed at five feet ten inches and 210 pounds. I had the 210 locked up, thanks to a lifetime diet of salty Italian meats and black-and-white cookies. If I could fudge an inch of height, I could maybe make it work.

So the *Kimmel* crew and I secured Media Day passes, headed down to Houston's Reliant Stadium, and patiently waited to see the Panthers in all their glory. And there they were, strolling out, proudly wearing their white road jerseys with black numbers and a light blue stripe across their sleeve.

Only problem was the jersey. We brought the Panthers' traditional black and teal home jersey. We had received some bad information (figuring both teams would have on what they'd wear for the game on Sunday) and, as a result, I was going to stand out even more than before. I guess we could've brought both the home and away jerseys in case of a mix-up like this, but, really, why spend an extra sixty-five bucks just to be safe?

I had to make do, so when the Patriots came out, and things became a bit more hectic, I bolted to the bathroom to change into my mismatched Panthers jersey and football pants.

We had the advantage of having our own crew with an ABC mic cube, so it would appear as if I were being interviewed by a legitimate reporter from a real media outlet.

Some of the bigger stations like ESPN and the NFL Network knew I wasn't the real John Kasay immediately. At one point Rich Eisen, who I was friendly with, passed by and gave me a look as if to say "I don't know what this is, but I know you're up to no good." Despite the fact that the cagey vets weren't biting, this charade ended up being a success. Several of the local news outlets as well as the foreign press approached me to ask questions: "How do you prepare for a game of this magnitude?" "What goes through your mind when you think about playing in the Super Bowl?"

I deflected all the cookie-cutter queries and talked about how it was all a blur to me, since I was out at the strip club until 4:00 a.m. I kept asking reporters if they could smell booze on my breath. I stated that I had planned to bet on the Patriots, so this was really a win-win for me. I told them I had a metal foot and that the league didn't know about it.

It was so great watching reporters without camera crews or recording devices scribbling my answers down furiously, as if I had just announced the Beatles were Nazis.

With a few minutes remaining for Media Day, we had decided we'd done enough damage and sought out the real John Kasay. Someone told us he was being interviewed in the stands, so the crew and I hustled over to greet him.

Me (to John Kasay): Ah…excuse me. What do you think you're doing?

Kasay half smiled and continued with his interview.

Me (to reporter): I don't know who you think you're talking to, but *I'm* the real John Kasay.
Reporter: Hey, will you get lost? I'm trying to work here.

I of course did not get lost and instead began answering the questions posed for the real John Kasay. Our responses overlapped and at that point, the real John Kasay wasn't amused.

John Kasay (to security): Can we get this clown out of here?
Me: I'm pretty sure you're the clown, pretending to dress up as me. How pathetic can you get?

Security began ushering me through the tunnel. Our cameras caught the whole thing and a piece of it aired on the local news. By midafternoon the reporters who got duped had all figured out the truth—except for the foreign press, who ran the strip club, drinking, and gambling stuff in its entirety.

We later found out that the real John Kasay, who was really tight with Jesus Christ, was furious about my off-color responses. The Panthers' director of public relations and the NFL PR guy also expressed their displeasure.

Word got back to ABC that I was forever banned from Media Day and would not be granted a credential under any circumstances.

I could understand the overreaction. We now send Jimmy's sidekick Guillermo to ask offbeat questions. My buddy Dave Dameshek goes every year and asks, "Is this a must-win game?" to confused Super Bowl–bound players, but back in 2004 shenanigans like this were unheard of.

Deep down I didn't really care. I could wear the lifetime ban as a badge of honor and it would look better than any media day pass.

And now for the part where I ruined the Super Bowl…

A few days later John Kasay became the goat for booting the ball out of bounds while kicking off in the final minutes of a very close game.

So there you go. I got in his head.

Who knows? Perhaps things would have been different had he let me do *all* his interviews and focused more on the basics. By the way, I bet the Panthers to win outright, so I guess in a weird way John Kasay got me back.

I DO MY PILLOW TALKING ON THE STAGE

Mike Tyson is the most feared and ferocious fighter of the last fifty years. Period.

We'll never see as intimidating a force as Mike Tyson in all of sports. That includes them all...warriors such as Roberto Durán, Jon "Bones" Jones, and my aunt Chippy after being told she can't smoke in a hotel lobby.

Tyson's intense predatory nature was the reason I bet on him any opportunity I could. In a weird way I felt like I shared Tyson's power when I backed him monetarily. I know it makes no sense, but I believed it, and betting on Tyson was cheaper than seven years of tae kwon do classes, so please just let me have my moment.

In the early days I would wager mostly against friends who didn't like Tyson. He was a polarizing figure, so I could sometimes find a few idiots who looked to strike it rich betting against the villain. But the truth is Tyson was such a dominant fighter that oftentimes I couldn't get anyone to take my bet unless I put my money on a first-round knockout. There were even times I would have to predict a KO in the first minute to have any takers. I specifically remember Iron Mike allowing me to cash in after making short work of Henry Tillman and Alex Stewart.

But it was really the fight against Michael Spinks that catapulted him into a different class.

I was only sixteen years old and had all my paper route money saved up to bet on the Spinks fight. I forget how I got the bet down—my friend's father or someone helped—but I remember having about $300 on Tyson, who was, miraculously, only a slight favorite. Spinks had beaten Larry Holmes twice by controversial decisions but was really a light heavyweight going up against the best big man in the game.

It was time for Mike (and me) to pounce. And we did. Tyson flattened Spinks in ninety-one seconds to become the unified heavyweight champion of the world.

The knockout punch was so hard, Michael's brother Leon lost three more teeth. (I promise this joke will hit harder if you google "Leon Spinks smile.")

That fight was over before it started. Spinks, like so many opponents, looked beat during the introductions. He had that glazed-over look in his eyes, as if a grizzly bear were about to check his prostate. He got paid $13.5 million and retired from the sport.

Mike took home $20 million—the richest purse in sports at the time—and I collected my $300. We all fared well that evening.

Here I am at age two, phoning in a last-minute bet on the Mets to my local bookie in Brooklyn.

Witnessing the birth of my children was cool, but nothing compared to pinning Santino Marella in front of nineteen thousand fans at the Staples Center with Cousin Jimmy and childhood hero Rowdy Roddy Piper by my side.

My degenerate friend Harry was able to score a job writing tickets at a sports book in Las Vegas only to be unceremoniously let go for unspecified reasons. As of 2020 he remains blackballed from taking any casino job.

My mom reached out to me after my all-you-can-vomit session in New Orleans. Her saying it wasn't funny hurt me the most.

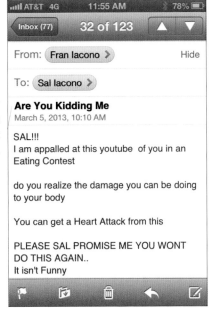

From: Fran Iacono ❯   Hide

To: Sal Iacono ❯

Are You Kidding Me
March 5, 2013, 10:10 AM

SAL!!!
I am appalled at this youtube of you in an Eating Contest

do you realize the damage you can be doing to your body

You can get a Heart Attack from this

PLEASE SAL PROMISE ME YOU WONT DO THIS AGAIN..
It isn't Funny

Scott Gagnon earns a place on Mount Oddsmore as one of my all-time-great degenerate gamblers. Little known fact: he's also a three-time *People*'s "Sexiest Man Alive" finalist.

If I remember correctly, about ninety seconds after this picture was taken, Aunt Chippy used the ladle to smack us both on the back of the head.

Me doing my best Jesse Orosco impression while throwing out the first pitch (low and outside) at Citi Field.

Moments before I was pickpocketed in the Black Hole.

The Undertaker in an unsuccessful attempt vs. the longest-reigning pillow-fighting champion in late-night television history.

My agent, James "Baby Doll" Dixon, took a break from his smoke breaks to pose for this photo with me, Michelle, and Barry.

I give you the most dysfunctional fantasy football league in America.

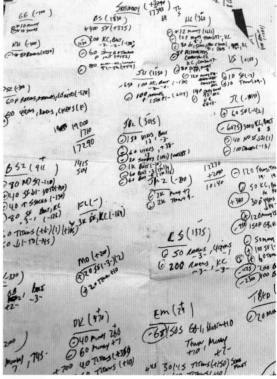

An old handwritten sports-betting tally sheet. Upon further inspection, I probably should have been imprisoned or at least institutionalized.

Todd Fuhrman, Clay Travis, me, and Rachel Bonnetta cohosting *Lock It In*—the first sports gambling show of its kind—on FS1.

My buddy Brad joined the navy to avoid paying his bookie. Nowadays he eats ribs at a furious pace in the hopes that, as he's choking on them, someone is around to save his life.

I don't deserve a family this good-looking. And they don't deserve being forced to root for the miserable Mets.

My parents are just as in love now as they were fifty-years years ago—assuming back in '68 they were on speaking terms only one week out of the year.

My grandparents, Sal and Edith Iacono. This is what a million bucks looks like. Notice the money in the background, too.

Me with my little sisters, Ivy and Teddi. Very proud to report that so far none of us has ever appeared in a sex tape.

February 11, 1990, however, was a different story. That was the night Mike Tyson lost to James "Buster" Douglas in what is still considered to be the biggest upset in boxing history. Iron Mike was undefeated in thirty-seven fights, and therefore Douglas went off in some casinos as a 42/1 underdog. In most other sportsbooks you couldn't even bet it. I, a huge Tyson fanatic, skipped watching and went out that night in Oswego, New York, where it was about −37 degrees.

That's how much I and everyone didn't expect Douglas to win, let alone compete. In fact, I've never even heard of anyone cashing a ticket for 42/1 on Douglas.

After the Tyson fight, Douglas did the right thing: gained forty pounds, lost his big payday against Evander Holyfield, and was never to be seen again.

Tyson was, unfortunately, never the same. He had a couple of decent matches with Donovan "Razor" Ruddock, then went to prison, then came back for some Mickey Mouse opponents such as Peter McNeeley, a terrible fighter who somehow landed a national ad campaign promoting terrible pizza.

And then came the Tyson-Holyfield fiasco. In their first encounter, Tyson fell to Holyfield in the eleventh round. Seven months later in the rematch, Tyson was so frustrated—or, as he would say, "fustrated"—with Holyfield's style that he ended up getting disqualified for biting his ear off... twice.

Yes, this happened. Holyfield had his lobes gnawed on while I had hundreds of dollars of bills chewed up and spit into my bookie's checking account.

My cousin Jimmy had no sympathy. This was a time to celebrate. The carnivorous combatant had provided comedy gold. I wasn't even done tallying my losses and Jimmy had come up with three solid radio bits involving Iron Mike's mid-fight snack.

I took a break from betting on Tyson after that and it was a good thing. The early 2000s were tough for him. He got bested by Lennox Lewis and was clearly on the downside of his career.

The good news for us is this downside coincided with the debut of my cousin Jimmy's late-night television show.

During the first year of *Jimmy Kimmel Live!* we'd have cohosts. A new celebrity would sit in Monday through Friday. We would try to have them do comedy bits to fill. Some notable cohosts were Adam Carolla, Kathy Griffin, Zach Galifianakis, Adam Carolla, Monica Lewinsky, David Alan Grier, and Adam Carolla.

It was exciting when we were able to book Mike Tyson for a full week. We had a lot of comedy planned with him. We traveled to his home in Brooklyn, where he showed my uncle Frank his pigeon coop. The piece was supposed to be a goof but turned out to be oddly inspiring and spiritual. We definitely saw a softer side of the most savage fighter to lace up a pair of gloves. Later in the week Tyson sang karaoke to a stunned Ali Landry. The next day we had him trading "yo mama" jokes with Jimmy while sucking on helium balloons.

I loved it all but was hoping the week would culminate with a pillow fight live in front of the studio audience between Tyson and yours truly.

It sounds ridiculous, and trust me, it is, but I was no pushover when it came to pillow pugilism. Swinging a piece of bedding at Tyson would not be my first feathered rodeo.

My pillow fights had become a comedy staple on *Jimmy Kimmel Live!* I squared off with the likes of Stone Cold Steve

Austin, Goldberg, and the Undertaker. And not just wrestlers: I did battle with boxing's heavyweight champion of the world Lennox Lewis. It wasn't long before I proclaimed myself the Pillow Fighting Champion of the World.

The matches were great. They didn't last long but they got the studio audience pumped up. Stone Cold really took it to me. He wasn't screwing around. I landed a couple of good shots, but overall the big Texan probably got the best of me.

The Undertaker was a fun but at the same time frightening one. In anticipation of the pillow fight, our executive producer and supposed friend, Daniel, was seen feeding him shots in the greenroom. Not my favorite managerial move by Daniel, but whatever loosened him up. When it came to the fight, I approached the Undertaker and said, "Hold on, there's been a mistake. I thought I was pillow fighting the gay undertaker from *Six Feet Under*...not the gay Undertaker from the WWE," and then tossed him his pillow. This angered the Undertaker and we battled for a good forty-five seconds before our pillows got tangled and the contest was ruled a draw.

Lennox Lewis was appearing as a guest with his mother and the late Anna Nicole Smith (think about that lineup for a second). The match was going well for me as I stunned Lennox early on with my patented pillow to the knees, then snap up to the head shot. Eventually his height proved to be too much and I became frazzled, grabbed a birthday cake on set, and tossed it, covering Lennox and his mom and Anna Nicole Smith with pink frosting.

That was only the beginning of the madness. After the bit, Lennox's henchmen tried to track me down. They weren't thrilled with the icing-on-his-mother thing. After the producers calmed them down, I still had to go into Anna's dressing room to apologize. Her weasel handler, Howard K. Stern, was screaming at me, saying I had run into her knee, which caused swelling. Only problem was her knee wasn't swollen and the tape shows I was never within three feet of her. I laughed through an apology and took off.

My pillow fight against Goldberg was the most memorable and the only one where I suffered lasting injury. The injury had nothing to do with actual pillow fighting.

It started off like the others. We felt each other out before I smashed the former WWE champ with a solid down/up combo. I felt that was enough and attempted to retreat and that's when Goldberg became angry and tugged at my shirt as I lunged backstage. The shirt eventually ripped, sending me flying into a curtain, and behind that curtain a four-inch nail sticking out of the wall and into my forehead.

The nail missed my eye by centimeters. My head was bloodied up. Goldberg felt terrible after the show, but I didn't care. Fifteen stitches and a scar was more than I could ask for. My wife was furious and demanded I quit this nonsense, but I reminded her that she had married a pillow fighter and that was that.

So now it was time to take on Tyson. By Friday morning we hadn't received word from any of the 319 people who claimed to represent him, so Jimmy took matters into his own hands. Right before the Friday show, he led me into Tyson's dressing room.

Jimmy: Mike, this is my Cousin Sal. He wants to pillow fight you on the show.

Tyson (unamused): I can't do it. I'll kill him.

Jimmy: No, he's actually good. He beat Goldberg and
Lennox Lewis and...

Tyson: I don't care who he beat. I can't do it. I'll kill him.

Jimmy: I don't know about that. We can show you footage of Sal...

This is where I, as the person thinking the second-most
clearly in the room, had to step in.

Me: I get it. It's okay. Have a great show, Mike.

I shook his hand and left. I understood. Even if I was a
better pillow fighter, Mike would become frustrated, eventually lose his cool, and resort to non–pillow-fighting tactics that
would potentially lead to my death. It was definitely something
he had worked out in therapy or with his tattoo artist. I don't
really care where it came from. I'm just glad he had the good
sense to say no.

Consider this a thank-you note fifteen years too late. I will
always appreciate Iron Mike Tyson for not killing me.

SCARIEST FIGHTERS
IN MY LIFETIME

CUSTOMER RECEIPT

Mike Tyson (-240)
Kimbo Slice (5/2)
Fedor Emelianenko (6/1)
Arthur McGee (seventh-
grade bully) (10/1)

Win total:

Total bet:

A CATCH-22

This chapter is the only one that doesn't have anything to do with gambling but there's an important lesson to be learned over the next few pages and that is meeting your heroes is a huge gamble. One that you should carefully consider before going all in.

I've been blessed enough to have the opportunity to meet some of my boyhood/early adulthood sports idols. Being introduced to Rowdy Roddy Piper and Cowboys quarterback Tony Romo couldn't have gone better. I'm still working on seventies superhero Shazam (not counting the drunk homeless guy in a Shazam costume on Hollywood Boulevard). The one that got away was Dallas Cowboys running back Emmitt Smith.

It pains me to tell this story but here goes. First, a little backstory. Attending college in the mid-nineties was ideal for a Dallas Cowboys fan. There was no better time to have bragging rights. In 1993 the Cowboys disposed of the Buffalo Bills by 35 points and then in '94 by 17. I was on top of the world and the fact that I went to school in upstate New York with a ton of Bills fans made it all the better.

The Cowboys' success was largely due to the legs of Emmitt Smith. Drafted out of the University of Florida, Smith made an immediate impact. In 1990 he scored eleven touchdowns. He went on to reach pay dirt 153 times in thirteen seasons. He's second on the all-time list for touchdowns—only Jerry Rice has more—and the number one all-time leading rusher—1,600 yards better than Walter Payton, who was widely considered the greatest in the game.

I was heartbroken when Dallas traded Emmitt to the Arizona Cardinals. I needed him to retire a Cowboy and not one of those bullshit rejoin-the-team-for-a-day things. He never should've left. He was a Cowboy through and through, and like I said, largely responsible for their dynasty years.

If there was a bigger Emmitt Smith fan than me, I didn't know him. I got into a ton of shouting matches with Lions fans and people who wanted to get under my skin by saying Barry Sanders was a better running back. I took it personally.

I bought all of his jerseys. I wore his number in varsity football. Emmitt posters. Emmitt mugs. Emmitt oven mitts. You name it, I had it. I was as loyal as an insane young man with a weird allegiance to a team that played in a city 1,500 miles from where I grew up could possibly be.

That's why the events of February 1, 2006, were so soul crushing.

It was a few days before the Seahawks played the Steelers in Super Bowl XL. *Jimmy Kimmel Live!* was doing a week of shows in Detroit, the site of the big game.

Jimmy Kimmel Live! went out there as a peace offering to the city of Detroit, which, the previous spring, had become furious with Jimmy for something he said during the NBA finals.

Jimmy joked that he hoped the Pistons wouldn't beat the Lakers in the finals because the fans in Detroit would burn the city down. Naturally, the Detroit natives were up in arms. Detroit is a huge ABC affiliate, so Jimmy had to apologize and then the unthinkable happened. The Pistons won the NBA title and the fans proceeded to burn the city. Two days' worth of fire and riot footage all over the news, but whatever: we didn't want any trouble with Detroit, and since ABC was hosting the Super Bowl, it made sense a few months later for us to go out there and make nice for a week.

The great thing about Super Bowl week is you have access to a lot of former athletes. We found out Emmitt Smith was in town and cooked up a hidden camera bit where I was to act as Emmitt's assistant and tool his fans. It was more of a make-a-wish thing for me than anything else but still had the potential to be a great bit.

So we reached out to Emmitt's agent and publicist through our sports booker. We sent them the premise along with beats detailing exactly what we would try. The idea was to have fans line up for Emmitt's autograph/picture. Once they got to the front of the line, I as his "assistant" would impose ridiculous limitations on what they could and couldn't do and see if they would play ball.

I would take the fans aside and say things like "Mr. Smith requests that you not make eye contact with him under any circumstances. If you're going to talk to him, he asks that you stare at the ceiling.

"Mr. Smith is very picky about clean feet. He demands that everyone wash their feet before posing for a picture."

One request would be more ridiculous than the other. This

would all be captured by our hidden cameras so as not to give away the gag. After they were pranked, each fan would be asked to sign a release and then actually get to meet Emmitt, take a picture, receive an autograph, etc.

It took less than a day for the publicist to send back a response email with the words "Emmitt loves this."

This shit was going down. I was not only going to meet the athlete who brought me the most joy in my young, pathetic adult life, we were going to be partners in a funny hidden-camera prank.

ABC sent out a press release inviting fans to come down and meet Emmitt Smith. The event was held at a convention center near Ford Field. Emmitt's people told us he would show up at noon and give us ninety minutes. It was all unfolding nicely. Too nicely.

I got there early with the crew on the day of the bit to see a hundred or so people lined up to meet the Cowboys legend. Shortly after, we got a message that Emmitt was running twenty minutes behind. No big deal: it's Super Bowl week; there's traffic. We weren't alarmed at all. And then he showed up in all his glory. Emmitt was not a whole lot taller than me but had a great presence. He looked like he could power his way through the Giants d-line right then and there. But he also looked preoccupied.

I was at video village—which is where all the hidden camera monitors were assembled—and could hear Emmitt talking to his publicist as he was getting mic'd up, reading a printout of the bit outline.

Emmitt: What is this? I'm not doing this.

Publicist (who had signed off on the bit): I don't know
what they have you doing here.

Emmitt: Good—'cause I ain't doing any of this.

Publicist: Of course not. You only do what you want.
We'll be in and out of here.

Uh-oh. This did not seem good at all. I thought maybe if I
introduced myself to him and told him what a big fan I was,
he would loosen up a bit. I approached him.

Me: Hello, Mr. Smith. I'm Sal Iacono. Jimmy Kimmel's
cousin. I'm playing the part of your assistant today.
I just want you to know I'm a die-hard fan of yours
and we're very happy to have you help us out with
this.

Emmitt (shakes my hand): Yeah, this is nice, but what
is going on here? I didn't agree to any of this.

Publicist: Yeah, we didn't know how involved this was.

What a fucking liar he was. The publicist knew exactly
how involved this was. The sheet of hidden-camera beats was
exactly the email he responded "Emmitt loves this" to. I had
to stay calm.

Me: Yeah, well, we forwarded you the ideas and you said
everything was good to go.

Publicist: You forwarded who the ideas? You didn't forward me the ideas.

This slimy shit bag was completely tossing me under the

bus. I looked around to see if the hidden cameras were pointed to me, because that's the only way this scumbag lying to my face was going to make sense.

HE SPECIFICALLY AGREED TO ALL THE IDEAS HE ALL OF A SUDDEN HAD A PROBLEM WITH!!!!

> **Emmitt:** Look, I don't know what is going on here. All I can tell you is I normally get paid $50 for an autograph, so this ain't happening.

So now it wasn't about the individual gags; it was the money he had a problem with. What the hell did he think he was coming to the convention center for? Did he think the mayor of Detroit was handing him the key to the city?

We went back and forth and eventually Emmitt relented... sort of.

> **Emmitt:** All right, you got ten minutes.

I knew that wasn't enough. That's not how these things go. You need twenty minutes to get rolling and then hopefully you're in a groove and so on. But, fine, ten minutes. I figured if we started hitting these marks with the funny premises, maybe Emmitt would begin to enjoy himself and give us a full hour.

We started with the first fan who was head over heels excited to meet Emmitt and did the "no eye contact" gag. This worked like a charm. Emmitt was asking the guy questions, and every time he responded, he remained staring at the ceiling. Same thing with the next mark who we had taking off his shoes and scrubbing his feet in a washbasin per Mr. Smith's "request."

Emmitt was actually laughing. Things were going great. And then like that it was over.

Emmitt: Okay, that's enough.

Me: Oh, c'mon, it's going great. This is really funny so far.

Emmitt: I don't care that it's funny. I don't do my fans like this.

Me (panicking): But there's no harm here. Everything's fine. They're getting to meet you after the gag.

Emmitt: I told you, I don't do my fans like that.

Me (pointing to the long line of fans): So you're just going to walk out on all of these people waiting to meet you? That's how you do your fans?

Emmitt (maintaining a stern look following a long pause): I said...I'm done.

Emmitt rips his microphone off his lapel.

Publicist: C'mon, Emmitt. Let's get out of here. And you people do not have our permission to air any of this. If we see a frame of this on television, there's going to be big problems.

It took all my power to not smash this dickhead publicist over the head with the used washbasin. I showed great restraint because I knew from our sports booker that this douchebag was supposed to help us get a player to appear with Jimmy after the Super Bowl. Which of course he did not.

I was devastated. After they left, I literally fell to my knees with my head in my hands like a game show contestant who lost a million dollars on a knock-knock joke. That really couldn't have gone worse. It was so ironic that the actual publicist turned out to be much more of an asshole than the over-the-top publicist that I was supposed to be playing.

I called Jimmy and told him the news. Not only did my sports idol hate me, but we were now short a comedy bit for the week. Also, we now had to manage a near riot as dozens of fans were told that Emmitt Smith had an emergency and was forced to leave. I have no idea why we covered for him. We should've just gone down the line and told people the truth that, despite earning more than $61 million over his playing career, Emmitt Smith couldn't deal with the fact that he had given away two autographs gratis.

As bad as it was, I came away from this miserable experience with three valuable lessons.

1. Always be careful what you wish for.
2. Publicists are among the evilest of people.
3. Barry Sanders was better than Emmitt Smith.

RIDING THE ROMOCOASTER

This next chapter is going to annoy people, but I promise it has a happy ending for everyone where I lose lots of money, so hang in there.

I am without a doubt the biggest Tony Romo apologist on this planet. And it doesn't really make sense because there's absolutely nothing to apologize for when it comes to TR's playing career.

I get that in the NFL, Super Bowls and playoff wins advance a quarterback to the upper echelon, but as far as I'm concerned—and this is the part that's going to irk people—Romo would've been remembered as one of the top QBs of all time if any one of three plays had gone ever so slightly differently...

#1.

The 2007 Divisional playoff game versus Seattle. Martin Gramatica lines up for a chip-shot nineteen-yard field goal attempt. Romo kneels as the holder, botches the snap, and then gets tackled at the one-yard line trying to run it in. I still maintain that this magic K ball was the shiniest rock in existence not residing on Pippa Middleton's finger. Not exactly sure where that stupid ball came from. Whatever...Not that this Cowboys team was going to win the Super Bowl that year, but this play stigmatized Romo in the eyes of the casual fan for a long, long time.

#2.

The 2008 divisional playoff game versus the Giants. For some mysterious reason, wide receiver Patrick Crayton slows down as a gimme touchdown pass from Romo sails over his head with fifteen seconds left in the game. The Giants prevail 21–17 and go on to win Super Bowl XLII when some no-name receiver uses his helmet to catch an Eli Manning duck.

#3.

The 2015 divisional round playoff game versus Green Bay. I don't even want to get into this. Four words. IT...WAS...A... CATCH. If Dez Bryant's reception is ruled correctly and the Dallas defense holds for one possession, the Boys are on their way to Seattle—a team they had already whipped—and quite possibly the Super Bowl.

You might consider one or all of these a stretch, but here's the bottom line: with the possible exception of playing center-field for the New York Yankees, there's no more desired position in American sports than Dallas Cowboys quarterback. And as an undrafted free agent, number 9 set all the notable team records taking snaps for this storied franchise.

Completions, completion percentage, passing yards, interception percentage, touchdown passes—you name it. In fact, Tony Romo has eighty-three more touchdown passes than Hall of Famer Troy Aikman despite playing in nine fewer games. So it really is senseless to argue his value to the franchise or the sport in general. Let's just agree that Tony Romo is great at a lot of things.

And perhaps the thing he's greatest at is convincing others to bet on him.

Tony—I'll switch to calling him Tony now because at this point in the story I've met and know him well—was never more sure of himself than in March 2018 when he earned an exemption into the Corales Puntacana Resort & Club Championship.

What the hell kind of golf tournament was this, anyway? Puntacana sounds like a swear word Rosie Perez yelled out the seventeenth time Woody Harrelson lost all of their money betting pickup basketball games in *White Men Can't Jump*.

All week leading up to the tournament, Romo was super-confident. And while he wasn't going to bet on himself, he continued to urge my cousin Jimmy and me to back him.

The first day Vegas posted his over/under at 74 strokes. We bet under. Tony shoots a 77.

That night he swears he'll improve. I explained to him that he didn't have to improve.

"You're not going to make the cut, so you should purposely gun for a high score... We'll bet the over... Everyone's happy."

Tony wasn't having it. These guys are too competitive. In fact, rather than participate in my fun scheme that could've potentially landed us in the same jail cell for a half decade, he urged us to once again bet the under. He had more confidence than ever—which was ironic, because Vegas had even less confidence in him than ever. Nevada casinos posted his Friday over/under at 77.5 strokes.

Jimmy and I did the honorable thing and doubled up on the under. This time out, Tony scored the number of his favorite target: 82. We lost again. Tony finished in last place at the bottom of the leaderboard—or, if you're a cup half-full kind of guy, at the top of the follower board.

"Puntacanaaaaaaaaaaaa!!!"

My sports idol punted my wallet. But this is where my cousin Jimmy shines, constantly turning lemons into lemon truffle sauce with lobster. He immediately went online, designed a "last-place" golf trophy, and shipped it to Tony's compound in Dallas.

We all ended up getting a good laugh out of it, especially Tony, who eventually came to realize that this award—of which there is only one made in the entire world—was a much more prestigious hunk of hardware than that piece-of-shit Lombardi Trophy.

Suck it, Eli!

NAILED IT

I'm not sure how interesting this chapter will be, as I'm guessing many people have been kicked out of a restaurant because an inebriated ex-athlete they once idolized was harassing a member of the Beatles, but I'll continue anyway.

I met Lenny Dykstra, nicknamed "Nails" for his toughness, back in 2016. He was an integral part of my favorite team of all time: the 1986 New York Mets. As a fifteen-year-old in New York, there was no greater feeling than rooting for the team that won the World Series and being able to rub it in with obnoxious Yankee fans. And had I known decades later I would work with so many Massholes, I would've cherished the moment even more.

Lenny parlayed his career baseball earnings into a financial empire. At one time he owned more than fifty car washes and somehow, using creative accounting and persuasiveness, finagled his way into buying Wayne Gretzky's $18.5 million mansion. He lost a good chunk of that empire after becoming addicted to private jet travel and, more important...gambling.

So therein lies the attraction, and the main reason I wanted to become best friends with Nails. I had heard and read many stories of how he might've screwed people over, but things were going too good in my life, so I was ready for a challenge.

Lenny and I had followed each other on Twitter and I invited him to a *Jimmy Kimmel Live!* taping. The encounter went off without incident, so when my friend Dave, maybe the biggest Mets fan I knew, came to town, I figured we'd take Lenny out to eat. I let Lenny pick the spot. He chose the Sunset Tower in Hollywood.

And now I digress. And I promise, it's worth it. Sunset Tower holds a special place in my heart. It's the site of my favorite dinner and potentially the greatest off-the-cuff joke I've ever heard. And it's all because of James "Baby Doll" Dixon.

● ● ●
● ● ●

It's not fair that I'm only going to spend a few paragraphs setting up James Dixon's existence. He deserves a *Lord of the Rings*–length treatment, but here he is in a nicotine-stained nutshell…

James "Baby Doll" Dixon has been my agent for twenty years. I met him through my friend Daniel when he was a producer on *Letterman*. He also represents a few arguably bigger names than me: Jon Stewart, Stephen Colbert, Adam Carolla, Bill Simmons, and my cousin Jimmy.

Before I torch him, I should say Baby Doll is a good-hearted throwback of an agent who does right by his people. I hear about other people's talent deals and how they are treated and it pales in comparison to how Baby Doll negotiates. In fact, he almost (according to him) brought the publisher of this book to tears negotiating my rate:

> I am going to hang up this phone and pretend I didn't hear that very insulting offer. My client doesn't pick up a fucking pen for less than three times that and you should be ashamed of yourself for low-balling me.

You're probably wondering why we call him "Baby Doll." Well, it's because *he* calls everyone "Baby Doll." He calls his daughters "Baby Doll." He calls his doctors "Baby Doll." He refers to the non–English-speaking busboys who refill his coffee as "Baby Doll." No matter who you are, you're "Baby Doll." This labeling of people "Baby Doll" has survived the #metoo era, because he doesn't mean it in a sexual way. Not that that matters anymore.

Baby Doll is an old-school cigarette smoker. There's a 100 percent chance he's polishing off a lung dart as you read this. His favorite joke is "You know how some people smoke two packs a day? I go through two lighters a day." It's a funny joke. At least, I thought so when the late Bill Hicks told it thirty years ago.

Baby is also a fan of Versace cologne, going through a bottle a week, every week. Trust me when I say the cigarette-Versace combo creates a dream scent that can't be duplicated.

Oh, and he's the last of the litterers. Baby Doll is not above dropping cigarette boxes and any type of trash wherever he is. He famously dumps bags of McDonald's outside his car window while driving on the Long Island Expressway. When challenged on this filthy habit and the damage he's doing to the planet, Baby Doll responds, "My name is Chuck and I don't give a fuck."

But my favorite thing about Baby Doll is his penchant for bragging about how much money he has. He'll constantly remind us with pictures of his vacation homes in the Vineyard and in Florida. All the private golf clubs he belongs to. The private jets he's flown in on. Baby Doll claims to be an expert on private jets, but when tested, he can at best identify them at a 50 percent clip. "Good thing I'm rich, Baby."

It's because of this arrogance that anytime Baby Doll comes to town and takes us to dinner, we—really my buddy Daniel and me—make it our mission to run the tab up as high as we can. We'll order the craziest kinds of lobster, champagne, drinks for surrounding tables. We always have the opportunity to do this because, as a result of his nicotine addiction, Baby Doll has to take twelve cigarette breaks during each meal. This allows us time to huddle up with the waiter/waitress and order all these extras before Baby returns. Inevitably, Baby will get the bill, throw a fit for a few minutes, and then start laughing. I believe we've driven a bill up to $11,000 for a table of six—and that was when we were generous enough to order the tables around us bottles of Dom Pérignon. I know it seems wasteful and people are starving, but trust me, Baby Doll deserves this, so just please take it for what it's worth.

Fast-forward to the infamous Sunset Tower night. Me, Daniel, Jimmy, our buddy Mike, and our pal Dicky. We ordered a lot of food...I mean *a lot*. Caviar, wine—all the regular expensive shit—and...robes. Yes, robes.

The Sunset Tower restaurant sits atop the Sunset Tower Hotel, so we were actually able to order bathrobes from the menu. That was a special treat and a quick $800 tacked onto the bill.

In addition to all that, we ordered three seafood towers. Every time he came back from a cigarette break, Baby Doll would see another majestic shellfish steeple. Comedian Jason Sudeikis walked by the calamity occurring at our table to say hi, which prompted this exchange:

Baby Doll: Jason, do you believe this fucking bullshit? These guys ordered three seafood towers?!
Jason: Three is a lot. Even the terrorists knew to stop at two towers.

The greatest, most terrible off-the-cuff joke of all time.

● ● ●
● ● ●

Back to the Dykstra dinner. This wasn't going to be a Baby Doll night. I was paying and wasn't especially excited about running up the bill on myself. Lenny sat with me and my friend Dave, who was like a kid in a candy store. Lenny eventually—and by "eventually," I mean immediately—said something off-color to our leggy blond waitress, who miraculously returned a few minutes later as a bald, overweight waiter.

The conversation was intriguing. Nails talked about hitting. He shared his theories on how some teams don't try during getaway games (a matinee game that ends a home or away trip). Dave and I enjoyed listening to him despite the fact that every fifteen minutes or so Lenny would throw in various business opportunities that involved me investing money. If I remember correctly, the deal was I would write Lenny a check for $100,000 and four or five days later I would receive a check for $150,000. I smiled and nodded and pretended to be interested while clutching my wallet the entire time. Who knows? Maybe I blew a life-changing opportunity.

Anyway, during the middle of the dinner, Lenny announced that he did a Facebook live hit after every Mets game and he was due to go live in a few minutes after the game ended. The problem was it was going to be difficult for him to break down that evening's Mets-Phillies game since we weren't actually watching it.

This gave me the chance to enable the Sling app on my iPhone and I streamed the rest of the game, bringing the evening to a new level of cool. Not only did Lenny play for the Mets but he also won a championship with the Phillies, so his rooting interest was all over the place. The analysis became more and more intense, as did the slugs from his flask.

The Mets, being the Mets, blew the game in twelve innings, and now it was time for Lenny—who at this point was a bit on the sloppy side—to do his Facebook Live hit. The plan was for me to shoot it with his phone by the pool area, which was a cool Hollywood backdrop.

Lenny set up, going over in his head what he was planning to say about the game, when, just before we start recording, he spotted one of the Beatles—perhaps the best Beatle, Paul McCartney—chatting by the pool bar a few feet away.

The night was about to take a turn and probably for the worse.

Lenny decided he was going to involve McCartney in his Facebook Live posting. Made sense. In Lenny's mind, the

Beatles played Shea Stadium in the mid-sixties so *of course*, once he made the connection, Sir Paul would be into this.

So now I had the unenviable task of spending the next ten minutes explaining to Lenny why it wouldn't be a good idea to attempt to involve Paul McCartney in his Internet recap. Lenny finally relented and we agreed on the following: I would record Lenny talking trash about the Mets' latest loss for a full minute and then, at the very last second, he would QUIETLY tag it with something like "even Paul McCartney agrees." I'd pan over to McCartney, who would hopefully not be looking in our direction, and that would be that.

I knew if we approached McCartney, he wouldn't agree to this plan, but it was the least invasive way to go about this, and thus our best option. Also, he would never ever know about it, so no harm no foul.

So what happened next? I pointed and began recording, and Lenny followed the script perfectly:

Lenny: This is Lenny Dykstra checking in from Sunset Towers in Hollywood. The Mets bullpen blew another game in Philly tonight and, check this out [loud voice] FUCKING PAUL McCARTNEY IS HERE.

I froze. I was not panning. This was not the plan. From there, Lenny continued to name check McCartney and it was only a matter of time before two security guards the size of Greg Luzinski ushered me, Lenny, and my friend Dave out of the establishment.

On our way out, Lenny yelled at me for not recording the

bewildered and bothered Paul McCartney while explaining to the bouncer that "Paul would be a fan of mine if he knew who I was."

Such a classic line to end a classic evening. As far as my relationship with Lenny goes, despite the near arrest, neither of us holds a grudge against the other. Ob-la-di, ob-la-da, life goes on...

BRAD BEATS

This chapter is dedicated to my buddy Brad. This will undoubtedly be the most entertaining section of this book. Brad should probably receive a portion of the proceeds for the sale of this memoir. On the other hand, I'll probably let him borrow money to replace his twelfth damaged phone this decade, so hopefully it will all even out.

Where do I start with Brad? Should I begin with the story of how he joined the Navy and spent more than 1,000 days on an aircraft carrier in the Middle East, all to avoid paying a local bookie $1,400?

Or maybe how his behavioral issues led to him being kicked out of multiple casinos?

Or perhaps we should commence with a retelling of a story about how he robbed gym locker rooms to pay gambling debts...

We'll get to all of that, but maybe it's best to start from the beginning, because the way Brad came into my life was nothing short of a magic story—literally.

Brad attended high school in New Jersey with renowned magician David Blaine. Even through all his fame and fortune, Blaine maintained his friendship with Brad because, growing up, Brad was one of the few people who stuck up for the introverted Blaine. Fast-forward to 1997. David Blaine is a giant success, commanding big bucks for magic shows and bedding down with young actresses and models galore (no thanks to Brad). ABC approaches Blaine to put together a show and pairs him with my buddy Daniel, who was hired to produce the special.

The idea was to shoot a few magic segments in Las Vegas, but it became a gigantic bonus when Brad tagged along to make his money and dignity disappear. In between takes, drunk Brad was losing hand after hand of blackjack, yelling at pit bosses and tossing drinks around the casino floor. My friend Daniel had seen enough. He did what every right-minded producer would do: he hired him as a production assistant on his new gig as showrunner for *The Man Show*.

That's where I met and fell in love with Brad. He was a no-nonsense (and yet all-nonsense) East Coast guy. As street-smart as they come, except when that street was one that he'd park his shitty Accord on in a prohibited space. This scene often occurred just outside our writer's room window. We would gather around to watch him berate meter maids who every day for a month, would ticket him for parking in a loading zone.

Back in the office, when he wasn't scrubbing the producers' refrigerator with a toothbrush, Brad tried teaching us Tonk. It was a gambling game he learned while he was sequestered at sea. I think it involved cards and some weird configuration of numbers. We never really got the hang of it despite how loud Brad screamed the rules at us.

But Brad's wagering interests didn't stop at Tonk. He knew he could get a bet in through me and I decided to let him play on credit. He was a character, and even though he was a filthy Yankees fan, I enjoyed talking baseball with him. So I would take his bets and forward them to my bookie in Long Island.

Brad played small amounts, $25 or $50, every day, all through the summer and then... you know how it goes. The house (not the one that Ruth built) always wins in the end.

It was mid-June and we were wrapping season one of *The Man Show* production, which meant Brad would soon go to live with his father somewhere near San Diego. He was into me for a few hundred bucks and looked to double up on the Sunday night game between the Braves and the Orioles. Brad risked what he owed me on the Braves, who ended up losing. Actually, it's not fair to call it losing. Cal Ripken had six hits in the game and the Orioles beat them 22–1. It was a shellacking. Any bookie in America would have been justified in collecting ten times the amount of the original bet, but I would've been lucky to get one-fifth of what Brad owed me.

I assessed the situation and there was a good chance I wasn't going to see him for six months or potentially ever. He owed me around $1,000 and, if he decided to ghost, I was going to have to foot the bill with the bookie. But then, like a David Blaine master of illusion, Brad showed up at the Hollywood Center Studios lot and squared away his account.

Years later, I found out how he came up with the money. Brad used an old trick he and his buddies learned while hustling in south New Jersey. They'd walk through a local gym locker room searching for open lockers, snatch a couple credit cards, and then head to a home improvement store. While there they'd use the stolen credit card to buy a gift certificate. Then they'd take that gift certificate and drive it over to another branch of the same store. There they'd purchase something insignificant, like a pencil, and get the remainder of the balance in cash. Policies have since changed, but back around the turn of the century they didn't make you show ID and didn't force you to take credit on a gift card.

So there you go. That's how Brad paid off gambling debts. It seems shitty, but Brad defended the crime saying it probably kept some competing mom-and-pop hardware stores in business for a few more weeks while making people smarter about locking up their belongings. (I know...)

This was all part of his routine. He didn't really have a choice. As far as his gambling roots went, Brad's ran deep. He recalls as a nine-year-old answering collect calls from prison, accepting and then writing down bets from the con man on the other end who happened to be friends with his father. His childhood was basically *Oz* meets *Crank Yankers*.

And so it makes sense that Brad would dabble in degenerate gambling circles. Like a lot of us, Brad would bet on anything. This went on for a good decade until it caught up to him. He had already filled out paperwork to join the Navy when he ran into trouble with his local bookie. Here's how he tells the story...

So, I owe this scumbag $700. It's Monday night football. And I'm, like, "Fuck it." I'm doubling up. So I have the Chargers over the Chiefs. They're the underdog, getting 4 and a half or 5 points...Doesn't matter. The Chargers have the ball late going in. They're already up 4. Natrone

Means doesn't get in. They kick a field goal to go up 7. If he scores, it's over, but his fat ass couldn't get in...so they kick a field goal. San Diego kicks off. Steve Bono has the drive of his life for the Chiefs—something like eighty-seven yards. I'm in the room. My college roommates know it's about to get bad. But I'm still getting 5 points in overtime.

Chargers, I think they got the ball first. It goes back and forth. Chargers punt to Tamarick Vanover, who goes maybe sixty yards for a touchdown. Chiefs win by 6. Fuck me. I am done.

At this point I've done this a few times. I told the guy I'd pay him Thursday. Wednesday, I'm in the Navy.

I mentioned earlier he spent 1,000 days in the Navy. Brad makes it very clear that he wants people to know that it was 1,095 days, including two all-expense-paid cruises to the Persian Gulf.

And those days came chock-full of highlights. Disciplinary proceedings, reprimands, gluing fellow sailors' lockers shut. Brad treated the Gulf War like it was high school on the high seas.

Perhaps his greatest military moment came when Secretary of Defense William Cohen paid a visit to the aircraft carrier. Brad describes work on the flight deck as loud, dangerous, and brutal—and that's coming from Brad.

So Secretary Cohen gets up there and bores the 3,000 cross-legged cadets with some praise and encouragement and then asks, before he goes on, if anyone has any questions. Each one of these poor souls has been told ahead of time that under no uncertain terms do they have questions for the secretary of defense.

Brad ignored the mandate. His hand shot up immediately.

Brad: Listen, Mr. Secretary...I've been working thirty-eight straight days. I'm a little concerned about my safety. We have a total of three channels here that only show *Martin*, *Basic Instinct*, and military propaganda, so your speech here will run over and over. There's not a CHANCE I will miss it. I'd feel a little more comfortable getting some rest.

Cohen: Certainly you may be excused. And anyone else who fears for his or her safety who would like to join this young man is excused as well.

Brad stood up to walk back to his quarters, and, just like in a scene from *Jerry Maguire*, no one followed. Brad didn't make it close to his rack before his superiors stopped him and gave him a tongue-lashing and a month's sentence cleaning toilets with a toothbrush.

He survived this tour with an honorable discharge, and I'm thankful that he did. I've had great times and greater laughs with Brad. We've gone to Vegas together a few times and he continued his streak of getting tossed out of various casinos in my presence. His go-to move is complaining to and berating the manager of the sportsbook for not having his preferred game featured on the big screen.

This, after screaming at the top of his lungs for five minutes about having bet on a "first to 10 points prop." If you've never been around a crazy person who has made this wager, you are really missing out. And if that crazy person is Brad, you are *really, really* missing out.

The idea behind the "first to 10" is you don't bet the entire game; instead, the wager ends once one basketball team scores 10 points. Brad placed a few of these bets over a weekend during March Madness and I can speak for everyone in the sportsbook when I say that watching him watch his bet was better than any game we've seen in decades.

When your bet is over in a few minutes, there's no reason to space out your intensity. And the intensity Brad displays is unmatched, because in his mind he's always in the living room of his studio apartment. I have to say, as someone who knows him, that it makes for top-notch entertainment. For others who have no idea who he is or that his bet is over in a few minutes when the score reads 10, it is a terrifying brush with a madman.

I swear every one of these games he bet the score was 9–8, with the team he wagered against in possession of the ball. Brad split on his "first to 10" bets, which was excellent news for his heart.

Speaking of his heart, I should conclude this chapter by pointing out that Brad has one as big as they come. During his daily walk to work through the roughest part of town, he's constantly reaching out to homeless people with a spare dollar or sandwich.

Brad currently works as a human interest producer on *Jimmy Kimmel Live!*, which is fitting, as he's the most interesting person I know. Brad is also one of the smartest people I know. I realize very little in the previous six or seven pages supports this claim, but trust me: he's as bright as they come. He's extremely well-read—he can tell you the cause of death of every British king and queen since the year 1400—and though he doesn't have a lot of money, Brad is a whiz at recalling and reciting great tales about financial empires and how they came to power and then crumbled.

He once broke the printer at work pumping out three copies of the Enron trial transcript. One copy of two-hundred-plus pages wasn't enough. He needed three.

I'm proud to know Brad. I'm proud of the fact that he's turned his life around. I'm proud he's gone seventeen-plus years without a drink and six weeks without getting slugged by a transvestite at a 7-Eleven.

Not sure if he's given a chip for that last honor, but he gets one from me.

GOOD NIGHT, JON HAMM

I have been playing fantasy football for almost thirty years, and I can say without hesitation that it's the greatest game ever invented. I mean, what are the other options? Monopoly? Jenga? Strip poker? None are even close to stacking up. In fact, forget about games. Fantasy football might be the greatest cultural phenomenon of all time. The idea that you can assign point values to real players in a fake league with all of your semi-legitimate friends can't be topped.

Having participated in leagues where entry fees range from gratis to several thousand dollars, I can confirm that fantasy sports is not about the money but instead about the bravado of being able to brag to your pals that you are more knowledge-able than them. When you break it down, after research, drafts, time spent thinking about moves, add/drops, and arguments over email, you are setting yourself up to win first prize at an average rate of $3 per hour. I know there are people who win a million dollars in high-stakes leagues, but for the most part you'd be much better off making macramé plant hangers from home than attempting to earn a living off of fantasy football.

I assembled my first fantasy football league in 1992. I was a junior in college and thought it would be a good way to make worlds collide between my high school and college chums. Harry, Larry, and Paulie from Oswego State would meet up with a bunch of my buddies on Long Island. We set up a weird and archaic format. A running back had to reach fifty yards to get 3 points. One hundred yards warranted 5 points. A quarterback didn't get points until he hit two hundred yards passing. This was before decimals were figured in. I'm not even sure decimals had been invented yet. We barely knew how to use round numbers.

I would score by hand. I took pride in it, but living on the East Coast was rough for the official tabulator. The results of the Monday night game wouldn't hit the local papers until Wednesday morning, which meant that oftentimes I would have to take matters into my own hands. I remember calling the *New York Daily News* sports editor on a Tuesday morning in the fall of 1994:

> **Me:** Hey, sorry to bug you, but can you tell me how many yards Haywood Jeffires had last night?
>
> **Editor:** Huh? Why?
>
> **Me:** I just need to know...I'm up against Mikey Mac and this comes down to first place in our division.
>
> **Editor:** I don't know what you're talking about, kid, but I'll tell you right now: Don't make a habit of calling me. Six receptions, seventy-seven yards.
>
> **Me:** Okay...thanks. One more thing...

Click.

He hung up before I could ask him about rushing yards. If Jeffires took a handoff and rushed for twenty-three or more yards, it would make a big difference. I called back a few times and the editor hung up each time.

I was not to be denied. I tracked the guy down at home, finding this poor son-of-a-bitch editor in the White Pages. I looked up the four names that matched his and later that evening, got lucky on the first try:

Me: Hello, is this the sports editor from the *Daily News*?

Editor: Yes, it is. Who's calling?

Me: Can you just tell me if Haywood Jeffires had any carries last night in Pittsburgh?

Editor: Let me tell you something, kid. If you ever call me at home again, I'll find out who you are and slice your balls off and feed them to your mother. You hear me?

Knowing my mother wouldn't love this, I decided not to call him again.

For the tens of thousands of you who are interested, Haywood Jeffires did *not* have a carry in that October Monday night game, and so I remained in first place after week three.

The technology in the fantasy industry (I know...sounds dumb) has improved vastly since the early nineties. I currently participate in four fantasy leagues. The one I spoke of earlier, the Elwood Football League—named after my hometown, where most of the team owners are from and some still reside—has been running with exactly the same group for almost thirty years. That speaks to how close and dedicated we are and also that our lives are a meaningless disgrace.

We have updated some of the rules and would love to eventually add some spice by switching from a snake to an auction draft. The difference between snake and auction is commonly compared to that between checkers and chess, but I liken it more to the difference between playing checkers and playing checkers with a bobcat tied to your neck. One is mindless and dull, while the other features several hours of nonstop panic.

Because the EFL is scattered all over the country, the only way to do an auction is to bid on players while everyone is simultaneously online. One EFL holdout who shall remain nameless (Frank Tassone) refuses to get a laptop. Frank actually claims he has one but it never seems to be in working condition around Labor Day, so this remains a joke Frank plays on the rest of us. It should be noted that Frank has only made the fantasy playoffs once this past decade, so I believe the joke remains on him.

Another league I belong to is modestly called the League of Leagues. It was created by two genius nerds named Toby and Jonah. It's a ton of fun but also a complete time suck. The League of Leagues includes three leagues: NFL, NBA, and MLB. You draft sixty players and get points for various categories in each sport. So it's not uncommon for LeBron James, Mike Trout, and Christian McCaffrey to go top five in a draft that seemingly goes on longer than the NHL playoffs.

The best (worst) part is that the trade possibilities are endless. In a regular fantasy football league, if team A and team B both need wide receivers, a deal will most likely not be made.

In the League of Leagues, there is always a trade in the

works. Team A can offer team B a wide receiver, a point guard, and a backup catcher for a tight end, a closer, and five NBA free agent dollars. It's pure insanity twenty-four hours a day, seven days a week.

I partner with my friend Brian, who was the former head writer of WWE's *Monday Night Raw*—which makes sense, because you really have to get banged in the head with a folding chair repeatedly to want to take part in something like this.

The third league I'm in is high stakes, involving my *Lock It In* cohosts Todd Fuhrman and Clay Travis, as well as other sports TV personalities and a few poker players who have all either cashed or won the World Series of Poker. The poker guys are nuts. I am both super-excited and terrified to befriend them. It's not enough that the buy in for this league is several thousand dollars. In addition to the hefty stakes, the poker pros will side bet each other just as much on their week 1 head-to-head matchup.

Last but not least is my West Coast fantasy league, which features the most dysfunctional assemblage of characters in the country. And I'm not just talking fantasy football–wise; I'm talking any club, religion, or cult. I'd like to say we're a motley crew, but we're more like Motörhead with less self-awareness. Lawyers, television producers, drug addicts, writers, womanizers, podcast hosts, and movie stars. Many checking off multiple boxes.

The ribbing on email starts off good-natured. But, as bad trade offers/trades pile up, the friendly give-and-take quickly pivots into shots about each other's failing careers, dead relatives, and much worse. We've often thought about disbanding, but we keep it together because I think we secretly enjoy the abuse.

Other than the indescribable hate text chains, there are two things worth noting that separate this league from the rest.

The first thing is the annual banquet. Every year the group gets together and settles their debts during the first game of wild card weekend at Shakey's Pizza in Hollywood. If you're not familiar with Shakey's, it's well-named. Their food is shaky at best.

On any given weekend one can pay a visit to Shakey's in Hollywood and come across a construction worker with third-degree burns on his face eating lunch, a Dungeons & Dragons tournament, or, if you're really lucky, a transvestite being jerked off in a corner booth. I have been fortunate enough to encounter all of them. The game we go there to watch usually features the worst playoff matchup of the weekend—almost always the game hosted by the AFC South winner. I'm pretty sure no Super Bowl winner has ever emerged from this subpar game we call "the Shakey's Bowl."

I'm not sure why we continue to frequent this seedy establishment. Most of us are fairly well-off. I guess the opportunity to make mojo potato jokes and the threat of trichinosis outweighs a good meal, so the tradition lives on.

What really makes this the best league is the kick-out rule. I'm happy to say I came up with this idea twelve years ago when we added a team and were stuck with an odd number of squads. Instead of adding a twelfth team, I suggested that we keep it at eleven and kick someone out every year.

This suggestion was met with much concern, but ultimately I prevailed and the kick-out rule became league law.

Here's how it works. Whoever wins the league has to kick a team out the following season in whatever manner he wishes.

The only rules are: you can't kick the team out two years in a row (the team that was ousted the previous year is always able to come back) and the act of elimination must be done live, in person, at the draft the following fall.

From early January through late August, who gets the boot remains a mystery. You can be knee-deep into research and a hundred bucks into fantasy draft kits, only to find out minutes before the draft you're getting the boot. (Now that I think about it, maybe this is what leads to the dysfunction of this league.)

There are some classic stories attached to the kick-out rule. First, as you might imagine, instant hatred is created. My friends Paul and Brad never liked each other from the time they met. Let me rephrase that: Brad disliked Paul even more than he dislikes most people and made that abundantly obvious during several brutal email exchanges.

Among other awful accusations, Brad accused Paul of not having said anything clever or funny over the last twenty years and wasn't afraid to throw the C-word around when Paul would attempt to retaliate. He would chastise Paul for "bad picks" during the draft and would ignore Paul at the Shakey's banquets.

No one knows what sparked this aggressive rivalry, but it made sense when Paul ousted Brad each of the three times he won the league. And even though he completely deserved it, Brad always took the low road on his way out the door. One time the door wasn't actually a door; it was a balcony at a sports bar. After being kicked out, rather than reenter the room in embarrassment (a few minutes before, in an act of disgust, he had poured Mountain Dew all over the floor), Brad shimmied his way down a makeshift fire escape and dropped to the ground.

Then there was the year my friend Elliot won. Elliot was an outsider and wasn't really buds with anyone but me. I kept him around because, when I moved out to LA, he was decent enough to let me in his league. He's a good guy, a nerdy and long-winded lawyer, and why wouldn't he be? In his everyday life he charges $400 an hour.

So, anyway, Elliot wins and now has the great privilege of ruining someone's football season. The rest of us had no clue how he would play this. What we did know was actor and fellow team owner Jon Hamm was running late that night. In addition to starring in *Mad Men*, on this particular day Hamm was directing an episode of the show. His shoot went a bit late so we waited an extra hour and a half for him to show up. When he finally did, out of breath from rushing over, he ordered a beer and was promptly sent home by Elliot.

Hamm downed his beer in a gulp and a half and, in very cool Don Draper fashion, bid us adieu.

I take pleasure in the kick-out rule, with the exception of the year it happened to me. My buddy Craig won, and when it came time to eliminate someone from the league, Craig announced that he was leaving it up to the rest of the league to vote on who would be sent home. This was not in the spirit of the rule, but we adhered to Craig's wish, and—in one of the great coups of the twenty-first century—I was voted out. Three people wrote down my name; the other votes were scattered among various assholes. But three was enough, and I made it my mission to get revenge.

It took two years, but my revenge was sweeter than fornication between a chocolate donut and a Twinkie. After winning the league the year after my return, I pitted those who voted against me against each other. Three teams of Tall Jon/Jamie (shared team), Dave, and Paul would have to fight to survive.

I set Dave to the side for the time being and had Tall Jon (representing his team) compete against Paul to see who could complete a puzzle quickest. This was only fitting, as the kick-out rule was inspired by the popular reality show *Survivor* and Tall Jon, Jamie, and Paul were the biggest *Survivor* fans I knew.

Opening the bag of puzzle pieces was a feat in itself as I had a weird triple knot thing going, and when they finally did, both were sweating. After five minutes the puzzle was about 75 percent complete. Paul was making a fierce comeback. Dave was rooting for him in the background: "Here comes the Mook," a name we affectionately gave Paul when he was a writer's assistant at *Jimmy Kimmel Live!*

Little did he know, Dave was cheering for his own demise.

Tall Jon and Jamie thought they lost until they looked at the Mook's completed puzzle, which read, "HASTA LA VISTA, DAVE...SEE YOU IN 2018."

A stunned Dave walked off in dismay. It was perhaps my greatest prank yet. However, it may have some negative consequences, as Dave gets the latest honor of kicking someone out. We shall find out my fate this September.

I should mention that Dave won the league last year after limping into the playoffs and beating me in the first round despite having lost five in a row and having scored 140 fewer points than me.

Like I said at the beginning of this chapter, fantasy football is the worst.

MOST ANNOYING FANTASY FOOTBALL PLAYERS

CUSTOMER RECEIPT

Forget to fill their weekly lineup (-250)

Take forever to pick during the draft (5/2)

Constantly offer awful one-sided trades (4/1)

Late payers (7/1)

My friends Frank and Brad (15/1)

Win total: _____

Total bet: _____

65988 - 4 4807802443545 379045345- 3 678 4534 3 -4 678 678353 678534

ANY WAY YOU
SLICE IT

I try hard not to let sports gambling affect how my children view me as a father. Every Sunday I take my three boys out to watch football, and rarely does a bad beat result in me (visibly) losing my mind. I can count on one hand how many times a full-on gambling-related temper tantrum occurred in front of my kids. It would be less than one hand, but somewhere along the way my bookie ripped off a thumb.

I'm aware enough to know you have to be careful with how you display emotions exhibited from bets that went south. It's one thing if I'm writing a book chronicling odd behavior stemming from gambling losses. It's another thing if thirty years from now my children are writing books chronicling odd behavior stemming from their old man's gambling losses.

Sports betting makes you do dumb things. On more than one occasion I nearly wrecked trying to sneak a look at a box score on an app while driving at top speeds in a car only to almost crash into oncoming traffic.

One time my twelve-year-old son responded with "What the fuck are you doing?" as I swerved to avoid a Prius. I totally deserved it, though our SUV was an 8/1 favorite against the Prius.

But a losing bet doesn't always manifest itself in tantrums or traffic accidents. Often it rears its ugly head in subtle, psychological ways.

Case in point: a recent Saturday in December. I had to navigate watching my oldest son Archie's wrestling tournament in a packed gymnasium while updating Big 12 championship results on my phone. I decided to wager heavily on the over in the Oklahoma-Baylor game. The projected point total was 66. I was feeling good about a big-time score fest. Baylor had put up 61 points the week before. Oklahoma's games went under the last two weeks, so they were due. (Notice how I illogically work both sides, backing both who is "due" and who is on a roll?)

The deciding factor was Oklahoma needed to impress the committee in order to get that fourth playoff spot. This meant that quarterback and Heisman hopeful Jalen Hurts would open up the offense. Also, my metrics (I read like two blog posts) told me that Oklahoma's defense was not as good as it had looked, so I expected fireworks from both offenses.

It was a tough watch between the whistles going off on the six mats in the auditorium and the whistle emanating from my iPhone after every tackle. For a couple hours I felt like a confused Chihuahua hearing other dogs bark on TV, but my professionalism prevailed.

My big bet was going poorly. The score was tied 23–23 late in the fourth quarter. Only 46 combined points. I caught a temporary break when the game went to overtime, which meant if each team traded a few scores in the extra sessions, I would be in good shape. Oklahoma scored a touchdown on their first possession—good. Baylor countered with a 4 and out—bad. Final score 30–23.

If I had bet the under, there would've been 172 points scored in overtime. But that wasn't the case, so I lost and was not in a terrific mood. Thankfully, my son was knocked out of his wrestling tournament early, and so we planned to meet the rest of the family at Joe's Pizza in Santa Monica, which was a few blocks away from the high school.

At this point I was calming down a little. Pizza will do that for me. One Sicilian square complemented by a slice of pepperoni and I'm on my way to achieving full degenerate wind down.

My wife arrived at Joe's early with my two youngest boys. When Archie and I got there, the regular pie—half pepperoni, half cheese—along with my Sicilian slice, was already sitting on the counter.

I polished off the Sicilian while updating my homemade gambling tally sheet. Then I scrolled through the Sunday games, trying to figure out which shit-bag pro team I could double my losses on. A few minutes later I looked up and there was one pepperoni slice and one cheese remaining.

Just as I was about to make my move, a homeless man stuck his head inside the restaurant. He asked my oldest son, Archie, if we could spare a slice. Archie didn't waste any time. I taught my kids to be charitable and, more important, to be afraid of people who looked like they could create a stir.

So Archie reaches over to hand the homeless man a slice of pepperoni. Out of habit and pure desperation, I blurted out the words "Wait a second, I wanted the pepperoni... Give him the regular."

Archie: Dad, what's the big deal?

Dad: No big deal. I wanted the pepperoni. Give him the cheese slice.

In a matter of seconds I was thrust into a *Curb Your Enthusiasm* episode. Although I'm physically more comparable to Jeff Garlin's character, on this day I was 100 percent Larry.

So now a family argument ensued, and of course no one was on my side. Also, somehow everyone in the twenty-foot-by-twenty-foot restaurant was now a spectator to this bizarre disagreement. An onlooker actually joined in. "You've gotta be kidding, man. Just give the poor guy the pepperoni."

At this point even the homeless guy was rolling his eyes. I know I'm not getting any sympathy here, but the way I saw it, this was an unfortunate situation but since I bought the pizza, shouldn't I get first choice on toppings?

I know this is the brain of a monster and it was all for naught, as Archie went ahead and handed the man the pepperoni slice. The guy thanked Archie and walked off into the Santa Monica sunset.

I took the L like a man, walked to the counter, and ordered another slice of pepperoni. Even the clerk shook his head in disgust. Why? I have no idea. I ended up giving everyone what they wanted and the business made an extra $4. The stink face seemed an unnecessary button to this puzzling experience.

But this story had a happy, more satisfying ending, as a couple weeks later I doubled up on the over in an NCAA playoff game. Oklahoma—this time I didn't need them to score as much—lost to LSU 63–28, and later that night I donated a good portion of my winnings to an LA food bank. Many needy people ate well that week courtesy of the Oklahoma Sooners and yours truly, the Pepperoni Prince.

BEST PIZZA TOPPING

CUSTOMER RECEIPT

Pepperoni (even)
Sausage (3/1)
Mushroom (5/1)
Pineapple (shame on you)
(700,000/1)

Win total:

Total bet:

65988 - 4 480780244354 5 379045345- 3 678 4534 3 -4 678 678353 678534

THE FIVE-YEAR PLAN

My wonderful wife threw me a big party for my fortieth birthday. All the characters in my life came out for it. It was like my funeral, but no one rented a suit and I was there to enjoy it. Lots of people from all different walks of my weird life met up, and I loved every minute of it. On the night of my party, my college buddy Ken got into a huge argument with his wife. The melee took place in front of a lot of people, just the way I like it. Ken tried to play it off afterward, but no one was buying it. In fact, my buddy Daniel bet Ken $500 he wouldn't stay married for another five years. Even though their chances of growing old together seemed bleak, Ken wasn't the type to back down from a bet, so it was on.

I don't think I'm being sexist when I say that only guys can understand this sort of wager. When one friend is facing a life-changing conundrum, the other makes it more traumatic by betting on it. It makes all the sense in the world to me. I mean, why sit and comfort someone, telling him everything is going to be all right when instead you can inspire him by betting on the demise of his marriage?

This one ended up coming down to the wire, and not because Ken and his wife's relationship blossomed; they actually hated each other's guts. But despite the fact that they slept apart and either didn't speak or fought every single day, Ken, for the sake of the bet, refused to file for divorce until after five years had elapsed.

Daniel, who was monitoring the situation closely, called bullshit on this and eventually I was asked to make a ruling as an impartial observer. Although I appreciated his dedication to the wager, I decided Ken had taken advantage of the situation and, in my estimation, violated the spirit of the bet. Therefore, I declared Daniel the winner.

Hanging on the extra few years while accumulating additional community property just for the sake of the bet likely cost Ken an extra $100,000 in the eyes of the court.

But don't feel bad for Ken. He will eventually get the money back somehow. In fact, he is currently suing his ex-wife's *lawyer's lawyer* for malfeasance.

And, yes, Ken and Daniel have a side bet as to who will prevail.

THE BOTOX BET

Sometimes the best bet you can make is one you can't win. Okay, that statement is ridiculous. Here's my attempt to explain just how ridiculous it is.

In the spring of 2010, my *Jimmy Kimmel Live!* office mates, writers Tony Barbieri and Bryan Paulk, and I thought it would be fun to wager on the NBA finals between the Lakers and Celtics.

The idea wasn't to risk money but instead humiliation and pain. Something tattoo-esque but maybe not as permanent.

It's important to know the gamblers involved. Tony is a great guy but a bona fide lunatic. You may know him as Jake Byrd, social justice "warrior" for *Jimmy Kimmel Live!*, who has appeared at various trials/rallies "supporting" the likes of Michael Jackson, Paris Hilton, and Donald Trump. He once crashed Rick James's funeral just for fun.

You may also recognize him as Mole from the cult classic *Windy City Heat,* in which he and comedian Don Barris mastermind a prank on one person. If you haven't seen *Windy*

City Heat, I urge you to put this book down and watch it on YouTube right this second. It's a great flick and I'm not just saying that because I'm in it.

The other participant in this bizarre wager is Bryan Paulk. Bryan is one of the funniest guys I know, a guy who is up for anything. We all shared an office. I'm actually convinced that Bryan suffered a little brain damage from staring at Tony's super-bright-orange ironic NRA poster splayed directly in his eye line, so anything he was about to endure with this wager was a walk in the park.

The three of us set out to bet against another office trio. Our initial plan was for us to take the Celtics. The three dudes we bet against would take the Lakers, and whoever lost had to do a cycle of steroids.

The problem was we couldn't find three coworkers to take us up on the idea. Turns out Hollywood writers are a crop of wuss bags who are terrified of becoming strong and muscular. So we decided to soften the blow a bit and say the losers had to get injected with Botox.

Certainly these sissies wouldn't mind the chance at a more youthful appearance? But still no takers, so we did the honorable thing and decided to bet against ourselves. After further deliberation, the dumbest thing we could come up with was that the three of us would get Botox injections only if the NBA finals lasted the full seven games.

The odds were in our favor. The finals had only gone the full seven games once in the previous fifteen years, so this was likely just going to be a humorous tease we could discuss around the office and our mothers and wives could yell at us about.

Despite being one of the great rivalries in sports, this Lakers-Celtics series turned out to be an unremarkable dud. The first four games weren't really close. Each game was decided by 7 points or more. The Celtics took game 5 by 6 points and had a 3–2 lead heading back to Los Angeles. If they won game 6, we wouldn't have to get Botox. If they lost... needles galore.

Of course, the Lakers ended up winning game 6 in a contest that saw 176 combined points. Game 7 was even worse. The Lakers won 83–79 despite shooting 32 percent from the field. Kobe Bryant, who went six for twenty-four in the final game, was named MVP for the series. It was almost as if the teams were trying for a game 8.

But it didn't matter who won. The series went seven games, so we lost. Now, the good thing about losing a bet to yourself is you can walk away and not pay up and no one would care. Not us three. It was time to find someone to inject poison into our scalps. I knew the perfect guy: Dr. Bruce. Dr. Bruce is like if Ichabod Crane came to life and passed his MCAT. Bruce is a good dude, always interested in your well-being, but he also has a weird side. I remember playing pickup basketball at Adam Carolla's, when I caught Bruce crying as he waited to enter the next game. No questions were asked. He wasn't the most stable doctor, but he was competent, willing, and free.

As if the stakes weren't asinine enough, the three of us agreed to get the procedures done on the upper deck of a Hollywood tour bus. In addition to sightseeing a Beverly Hills mansion the guide would tell you once belonged to Lucille Ball, tourists would catch a glimpse of a doctor injecting toxins into the forehead of three grown, stupid men.

Bruce pulled out of the bus stunt at the last minute, saying it would be too dangerous. We protested, but he insisted that if the bus hit a pothole, one of us could go blind.

Yelling at Dr. Bruce, urging him to inject us with botulism on a tour bus, was a new Hollywood low. Not just for me but for anyone. And that's saying a lot, as I've seen a homeless man dressed as Spider-Man attempt to urinate on a woman handing out samples in front of a Wetzel's Pretzels.

We regrouped on the second floor of the Hollywood Hooters to come up with a new plan. As luck would have it, we found out afterward that there was a robbery downstairs. The guy made off with eleven thousand chicken wings and sixteen stalks of celery.

Actually, I'm not sure how much the thief got, but I do know being murdered at a Hooters while planning on how we were going to pay off a Botox bet we lost to no one would've been the absolute, most perfect way for me to perish.

We settled on doing it on top of a building near *Jimmy Kimmel Live!* Each of us would get three shots of onobotulinumtoxinA into our foreheads. If you care to view the results go to YouTube. The video is under "Botox Bet.mov." I'm the fat idiot in the brown shirt.

I have to say, the anticipation was worse than the actual injections—although I did feel dizzy for about an hour afterward. Still, I don't know how the Kardashians do this every day. I'd love to know which stupid NBA bets they're making (besides marrying Lamar Odom).

DON'T PASS DAVID

Celebrity chef David Chang has been listed as one of the "75 Most Influential People of the 21st Century" by *Esquire*, one of the "Most Creative People in Business 1000" by *Fast Company*...and now "a real goddamn mensch" by me.

I barely knew the host of Netflix's *Ugly Delicious* when he offered to host me, my friend Bill Simmons, and our wives (and glutton Joe House) in Las Vegas at his Momofuku restaurant in the Cosmopolitan.

The salt-and-pepper lobster shrimp, the Snake River Farms Wagyu bavette, the five-spice roasted duck. It all made for the undisputed greatest birthday meal I ever had in my life.

After dinner, it was off to the tables. Blackjack was everyone's game, so we headed downstairs.

Simmons and I gave the dealer cash. "Change, $500!" The pit boss barely made eye contact with the dealer and we were given our chips.

Now we waited for Chang to get his marker. He handed them his ID, which was passed along to the appropriate authorities, who gave him a good look up and down. The important person holding his ID left, came back, and said there was a problem verifying his credit, which would cause further delay.

Just to clarify, David Chang has the most popular restaurant in the casino, and maybe all of Las Vegas, and they weren't taking his ID.

Chang played it cool for ten minutes before stating the obvious: "My face is on the fucking chips!"

It actually was. There was his smiling head right smack in the middle of a $25 chip, and in real life he was miserable that they wouldn't let him play on credit.

Finally, the casino manager gave in and accepted his ID, and we started playing. And then the inevitable crushing began.

Every hand, the dealer dished out threes and fours while showing kings. And occasionally when she didn't have a winning face card, she'd flip over a five-card twenty. This went on for a good hour until the three of us were out of cash, markers, and David-face chips.

By now I was used to this. Blackjack has been kicking my ass my last dozen trips to Las Vegas. It gets me crazy, because I'm a technically flawless player. It's not hard. I stay when the dealer has shitty cards, go after it when they show a seven-plus. Never take insurance, split and double when the book says to, and yet I don't think I've won three hands in a row this decade.

I know people have their superstitions, but I don't blame the dealers. Here's why. Every dealer has to play by exactly the same rules. That's all you need to know. Forget all your biases. It would be different if female dealers from Beijing were allowed to hit on eighteen, whereas male dealers from Chicago had to stay. Getting mad at blackjack dealers is like screaming at your exterminator about the termites. Not to mention—and this is very important—YOU GET TO CUT THE CARDS.

So, unless there's a vast casino conspiracy far beyond the confines of logic, I'll continue to maintain that it doesn't matter who's flipping over the cards.

Also, it's hard enough to find a blackjack table with one spot open, let alone three for you and your buds. You have to sit together, because God forbid you sit separately and reconvene in a few hours with exactly the same story of how you won, won, won, and then doubled up and lost and then kept losing. What fun would that be if everyone couldn't witness the same thing that happens every single time?

My biggest problem is with the friends I play with. I enjoy playing most with Bill and Daniel, although their commitment to a specific table varies wildly. Daniel has a system where if he loses three hands in a row, he bails. No questions asked. It's a tiny bit antisocial if you're there with a group, but I get it. In Vegas, self-preservation is a commendable trait.

Bill is on the opposite side of the twenty-one spectrum. He will play all night at the same table and will refuse to leave until they implode the casino and turn it into a Wet'n'Wild. And even then, if he's on a heater, he might weather the dynamite and play through. I've been with him until 5:00 a.m. where he's literally been asked to lift his feet so they can vacuum. I admire his dedication to the game; the only problem is, unless your last name is Musk or Zuckerberg, you can't be on a terrible run and hang with Bill.

Which begs the question: How long are you required to keep losing before leaving a friend stranded at a table alone?

On one hand, you don't want to be called a dick for leaving him behind, but you also would like at least one of your three children to be able to go to college.

Blackjack sucks and I need a new game. None of my friends will ever play poker or craps. Except on this evening, when David Chang was my savior. He convinced Bill to leave the losing blackjack table to toss dice.

I'm not sure why more people don't love craps. It's the game with the best odds, and in all the Indian casino commercials it's the game where people are having the most fun. Latina woman with expensive jewelry throwing her arms in the air while rich guys rejoice...I'm in!

I think people are intimidated by craps. They shouldn't be. The dealers are helpful. They'll tell you exactly what's going on. I like betting the point (the number the player hits on his/her opening roll), backing odds behind the point, and then the six and the eight. But even that can get boring, so I am willing to go against the grain and try the David Chang method.

Chang likes betting "Don't pass," which means you're rooting against the roller and pretty much everyone at the table.

His line of thinking is the house always wins, so if you have a chance to be the house...be the house!

Imagine if in blackjack you were allowed to deal. Similar reasoning here.

Betting the "Don't pass" line is the ultimate heel move. And I have no problem betting against the good guy. My favorite NCAA tournament wager is that there will be no buzzer beaters in the Thursday/Friday games. People say I'm not appreciating the most exciting part of the game. I disagree. The ball goes up in the air with no time left and I'm just rooting for it to clank off the iron. There will still be one team celebrating, right?

Despite what the Pechanga Morongo commercials will have you believe, it's not about having fun; it's about winning.

So Chang and I bet against the table and were quietly (not quietly at all) celebrating when the rollers on the other end of the table crapped out. This got in their craw, so when it was time to roll, they would aim for us. They were literally chucking the dice in an effort to hurt us. And when it was our turn to roll, we would do the same.

These hotheaded fellas at the other end of the table seemed to be of Russian descent. They went on some kind of winning streak. They must've rolled for twenty minutes straight. Chang and I bet against them every one of those minutes.

We left with empty wallets and little square welts all over our arms. Vegas, baby!

WORST PLAYER AT BLACKJACK TABLE

CUSTOMER RECEIPT

Hits on 16 against a 3, 4, 5, or 6 (even)

Is a smoker (5/2)

Berates the dealer when he loses (4/1)

Doesn't tip after winning several hands in a row (5/1)

Takes more than 10 seconds cutting the deck (There's no skill to this.) (6/1)

Win total: _____

Total bet: _____

65988 - 4 4807802443545 379045345- 3 678 4534 3 -4 678 678353 678534

A LOSING PROPOSITION

Each year, $350 trillion is wagered on the Super Bowl. I know, the number seems a little high, and that's probably because I made it up, but you can't challenge me on it. There really is no way to accurately predict the amount of money wagered world-wide on the Super Bowl. I'm pretty sure there isn't a pollster hovering outside a basement in Hell's Kitchen, counting all the prop parlay money neighborhood degenerates are flashing the week leading up to the big game.

Almost any number would make sense. The Super Bowl is a spectacle that 100 million viewers tune in to see (that number is at least close to accurate) and offers a bevy of ways to bet.

The most common way to bet on the Super Bowl is to buy a square. Typically you divide a piece of poster board into one hundred boxes and draw random numbers. Some numbers like 2 and 5 are dog shit, because you rarely see a game or quarter end 22–15 or 32–25. But theoretically everyone purchasing a square whose number is randomly determined before kickoff, has a 1 in 100 chance at winning. Obviously, the more squares you buy, the better the chances you have at getting the good numbers…blah, blah, blah. Squares pools put everyone on an even playing field. The nerd girl in Accounting who doesn't own a television set has just as good a chance at winning a squares pool as idiots like me who haven't missed a snap since God took Sunday nights off.

I'm not a tremendous fan of the squares pool. For the last few years we've watched the Super Bowl at my friend Adam Carolla's warehouse. Let me say this: if you're forced to view a Super Bowl in a warehouse in Glendale, California, Adam Carolla's is the one. It's got everything: food, thirty-seven TVs, and even more of Paul Newman's race cars. A man-child's delight. We usually have about forty or fifty people show up.

Before the game I am always very busy juggling prop bets and bracing myself for the eventual postpartum depression that sets in once football season is over.

On top of this, I have to deal with people who know nothing about football, usually the relative of a friend or something. This is a typical Super Sunday conversation.

Know-nothing fan: Hey, Sal, I'm thinking of placing a bet. What's the spread today?

Me: Patriots minus 3.5.

Know-nothing fan: So you're saying they can lose by 3.5 points?

Me: No, I'm saying if you bet on the Patriots in order to collect money, they would have to win by 4 or more points. If you want the Rams, they can either win

the game outright or lose by 1, 2, or 3 points for you
to collect.

Know-nothing fan: So, what if I bet both the Patriots
and the Rams? Then I can't lose, right?

Me: Excuse me one second while I go dunk my head in
a hot vat of chili.

The hours leading up to the game focus on me dealing with
time-sucks like this and helping whoever is in charge of collecting money for the squares pool. It's always the same deal. We
need $1,000 to fill one hundred ten-dollar squares. A few min-
utes before kickoff we'll have, like, $850, and then my cousin
Jimmy, my friend Daniel, and I will buy up the rest. Then we
assign numbers and sit back and watch as the kid whose father
bought one square and spent four hours on his iPad without
once glancing up at the Super Bowl wins the big prize. God
bless America!

But the squares pool doesn't do enough to quench the thirst
of a degenerate football bettor like me. Luckily, the Super Bowl
now offers upwards of five hundred propositions on the greatest
spectacle in sports. Anything that has anything to do with the
game that can be quantified is for the taking.

I have spent dozens of adult hours on the toilet scouring
the list of props, which reads like the menu at a Cheesecake
Factory.

It is your job to look beyond the bistro shrimp pasta to find
the white chocolate raspberry truffle.

When it comes to Super Bowl propositions, the offshore
(illegal) accounts are more liberal with their offerings. Some
betting houses are more playful than others.

I like to lose as much money before the game starts as possible. That's why betting on the National Anthem is a perfect go-to prop for me.

Yes, I'm the idiot holding a stopwatch by the big screen, making sure Pink holds out for longer than a minute and fifty seconds. Incidentally, you can also bet what color hair Pink will have and whether or not she will botch a word and just about any Pink activity so long as handicappers can hang a number on it.

This over/under bet on anthem time is not made by me without due diligence. I definitely check YouTube to time Pink performing the anthem in the past. I try to get inside info from publicists who may have witnessed the rehearsal. And then ultimately it comes down to the director cutting away to show the fighter jets flying overhead as Pink holds the word "brave" from anywhere from three to twenty-three seconds. How do we call that one? It remains a mystery and in the hands of whatever betting service determines the result, in some cases as late as the following day.

The coin toss is fun and it's especially telling that the online sportsbooks continue to take vig on both heads or tails. That's all you have to know about how impossible it is to win at gambling. The house collects EXTRA MONEY for a dead-on 50/50 bet. Thinking about it, I now feel really stupid about writing a book glorifying gambling and making you pay for it.

And then there's the halftime show. One time I wagered money on "Will Pete Townshend smash a guitar at any point during the Who's halftime performance?"

I, of course, went with "Yes." I mean, why wouldn't he? The Who is a top five badass band of all time. Pete Townshend used to smash guitars at small pubs in Birmingham in front of a crowd of three hooligans. This time he has the whole world watching him.

When Townshend finished "Won't Get Fooled Again" he carefully put his guitar back in the stand as if he were placing a Jenga piece on a tower. Guess who won't get fooled again? Me. Mark it down: I'm never betting on anything Pete Townshend does for as long as I live or he lives. Maybe I'll just bet I outlive him.

How many times will Deflategate be mentioned? What color tie will Joe Buck wear? I've seen some books post a prop where you can bet on the race of the first player who scores. I'm not sure how that one is calculated. If ethnicity is in question, I imagine you can issue a challenge and a 23 and Me representative will administer a test before the extra point is attempted.

And after the game you can bet on who the MVP will thank: coach, wife, God.

THESE ARE ALL FAIR GAME!

And then there's the postgame Gatorade dump. I believe the first time a pro football head coach was dumped on in a celebratory fashion was when the Giants did it to Bill Parcells in the 1985/1986 season—which is hysterical, because he's as no-nonsense a coach as they come.

The Gatorade dump isn't all fun and games. Legendary NFL coach George Allen said he wasn't feeling well after his Long Beach state team doused him with ice water. Allen kicked the bucket six weeks after his team emptied the bucket. So not always good times, but this didn't stop a bunch of online books from putting odds on what color the liquid in the bucket would be.

Clear is always the most popular option. The winning team's uniform colors are usually second and third. I used to bet my friend Daniel on this. For many years it went down without incident, but then one season Bill Belichick was christened with blue Gatorade and Daniel spent the next three days trying to convince me there was a tinge of green.

When Daniel is not being a pain in the ass trying to color match the Gatorade hue, he likes going for the long shots. It's happened more than once that he's endured an entire season of losing only to bounce back to make a big score on a bet of great odds.

Case in point—something my Uncle Frank preached for many years: "Safety first." Only in this case it means that the first score of the game would be a safety. This prop usually goes off at 40/1 odds and Daniel is all over it.

In fact, he was jumping up and down when Tom Brady was flagged—I know, right... it seems impossible—for intentional grounding in the end zone, giving the Giants a safety and a 2–0 lead. Daniel is a huge Patriots fan but an even bigger fan of winning crazy bets, so people were a little confused when they saw him in full Kool and the Gang celebration mode after the Giants took the lead.

Daniel struck lightning again a few years later when Peyton Manning crumbled in the end zone against a spirited Seahawks defense to start the game. The weird thing about the odds for a safety being the first score is they didn't change. I always thought 40/1 meant this happens 1 out of 40 times, but the gambling algorithm apparently doesn't adjust even if the safety hits five years in a row.

Cross-sport props are fun, too. For instance, "Tiger Woods

fourth-round score in the Waste Management Classic vs. Randy Moss receiving yards."

Just in general, I like to be able to say I wagered on the Waste Management Classic. Seems like a good way to describe how I spend most of my time.

Kyrie Irving total points vs. Cleveland vs. Seahawks points in the Super Bowl.

Manchester United goals against Liverpool vs. Eagles turnovers in the Super Bowl.

With dozens of other sporting events going on in a given weekend, you can imagine the permutations. I usually stay away from these, mostly because I think it detracts from how special the Super Bowl itself is, but also because trying to figure out how many penalty minutes the Flyers will incur vs. John Madden's halftime bowel movements gives me a headache.

Probably my proudest prop bet accomplishment came about ten years ago. It wasn't a prop that I won a lot of money on. In fact, I lost.

The Gary Russell Special originated on Bill Simmons and my *Guess the Lines* podcast. Every year, as we review our favorite Super Bowl prop bets, I try to make one with the most bizarre and uninteresting outcome involving an obscure player. Giants fullback Henry Hynoski and Patriots tight end Michael Hoomanawanui have each been served this distinction. I usually bet the over and it usually takes five or six yards to win this prop. The no-name player typically has one shot at glory.

When the Steelers played the Cardinals in Super Bowl XLIII, I had a few third stringers to choose from and, after a fake drumroll, I revealed my Inaugural No-Name Prop Player to be Steelers running back Gary Russell. The online sportsbooks had placed his number at –150 to *not* score a rushing touchdown. That means you had to risk $1.50 to win $1 if you thought Gary Russell wouldn't score. And I had a lot of dollar fifties saying that he wouldn't. Russell had three TDs in twenty-seven career games. And only three in fifteen with the Steelers. Not the kind of guy you trust at the goal line in the biggest game of the year.

Gary Russell was a fine backup—but I looked it up and Keri Russell had more touchdowns. So I concluded he wouldn't figure into the scoring.

Well, not only did Gary Russell score a touchdown, he scored the *first* touchdown of the game—a proposition that would've paid over 40/1 in most books.

But that's not the cool part of the story. A few months later Simmons gets an email from someone claiming they were at a Super Bowl party. When Gary Russell scored, the guy immediately laughed, thinking back at my ridiculous prediction, and while doing so he noticed a strange woman a few feet away doing the same. He approached the woman and confirmed that she was a *B.S. Report* listener and was also gleefully acknowledging my misery.

The two struck up a conversation and eventually got engaged and then married. I'm guessing not all in the same night, but it's cool to think that I was able to bring two people together in holy matrimony and that, along with Gary Russell, they were both able to receive rings as a result of my horrible Super Bowl prop bet.

GREATEST SUPER BOWL
ANTHEMS

CUSTOMER RECEIPT

Whitney Houston
(-10000000)
Field (1500/1)

Win total:

Total bet:

65988 - 4 4807802443545 379045345- 3 678 4534 3 -4 678 676353 678534

THE BOBBY KNIGHT OF ELWOOD, LONG ISLAND

Growing up in Long Island in the eighties was defined by three things: girls with ridiculous hair keeping the Aqua Net brand alive, great pizza with pepperoni that curled up into tiny cups, and an Off Track Betting in every town.

Off Track Betting, otherwise known as OTB, is best described as a racetrack stuffed into a 1,000-square-foot cigar box.

One of the great gambling scenes in movie history occurred in *A Bronx Tale*. (Apologies for yet another *Bronx Tale* reference but it's a great goddamn movie.) Crime boss Sonny LoSpecchio, played by Chazz Palminteri, and his underlings are at the track rooting for a horse they bet big money on. The horse, Kryptonite, seemed to have the race in hand, when all of a sudden local loser Eddie Mush emerges audibly rooting for the same horse. Mush was known for losing every bet he made, which prompted Sonny and his cronies to rip up their tickets BEFORE Kryptonite lost the race, which, of course, he did.

Anyway, OTB had all the elements of this *Bronx Tale* scene. A group of poorly dressed, unlovable Mushes. It was like a group of Homer Simpsons (and likely one or two OJ Simpsons) gathered in a miserable room to lose their paychecks.

No one at OTB ever seemed happy and yet, settling in to wager on a few simulcast races in a smelly confined area was probably better than anything any of them had going at home.

But the best aspect of OTB was that the people in charge didn't seem to give a crap about age requirements.

That's where sixteen-year-old me came in. I liked following the ponies. As a teenager, I loved the idea of betting on horses as well as the idea that an animal gives a shit about if you bet on him. It all spelled D-E-G-E-N-E-R-A-T-E in capital letters. *Newsday* had all the results from the previous day. I would study them and a few days a week I would also watch the replay of the races on SportsChannel. Harvey Pack was a tiny bald man who hosted a show called *Inside Racing*. I got a kick out of him, especially his sign-off: "May the horse be with you." There's an excellent chance Harvey wasn't even aware that he was making a play on the *Star Wars* slogan, but before that he'd set up the races and say a little bit about the horses. I found it to be very beneficial. I would try to predict the winner during the rebroadcast of the race.

My goal was to hit an exacta, usually a big favorite combined with a medium-range long shot. Sometimes exactas paid good money, especially when you were home alone, watching on television, and not actually betting. The big test was applying it to real life, with real-lifers at OTB.

You're not going to believe this, but I wasn't nearly as successful in a practical setting. I only remember winning once in a three-summer span. I had my paper route money on an exacta that paid 25/1. When it hit, that served as the only day of the summer that my gas tank was full.

My favorite OTB memory came one August when I ran into a local legend. Jack Mack coached our high school soccer team to multiple state titles and our basketball team to several county championships. He himself was a Hall of Fame athlete at Hartwick College.

Coach Mack could hold court for hours in a very loud and commanding manner. The students and faculty were endlessly entertained by his stories. Well, not all the students.

I had the pleasure of taking Mack's business law class. He had a unique way of conveying his lesson plan, which was mostly screaming. And when it came to giving out grades, Mack wasn't shy about announcing your test score in front of the entire class. He would literally announce the scores from highest to lowest.

Chat, you got a 68. 6-8...not a bad height—but a shitty score.

Chavkin, 64. Do us all a favor and try to save your drinking for the weekends, not the night before the test, will ya?

Marsh, 61...Maybe we should send you off to a special ed class.

Mack took no prisoners. And if you mouthed off to him, you almost immediately regretted it.

So now we were a couple summers removed from that class and I was at the OTB with Mack in my sights. Mack was alone at a stand-alone table. He had his head down, which meant nothing. He always had his head down. Everyone in the place was looking down, which was why sixteen-year-olds went unnoticed in the first place. I approached the Bobby Knight of Elwood.

Me: Hey, Coach Mack. You got a tip for me?

I knew he played the ponies a lot and even heard that he had a system. Knowing Mack, I figured he loved being right, and so whenever he could school anyone on anything, he wouldn't squander the opportunity. I was ready for a brief lecture accompanied by a winning horse. Mack, consistent with the surrounding clientele, continued to stare down at his race card and in a mild, but stern voice said:

Mack: Yeah, I got a tip for you. Get the fuck out of here.

It was probably the best tip I could've received. I didn't listen, of course. I stuck around and picked my own losers...but still, good, solid advice. And it made for a fun anecdote with my pals, one of whom was Mack's son, Mike, who got a big kick out of the story. Some years later Mike Mack and I actually teamed up to—you guessed it—book football bets. And not just any football bets: football bets made by my fellow law school classmates. We did very well, because it turns out Eddie Mush comes in many forms.

A PRICKLY ROSE

I have a popular sports gambling podcast called *Against All Odds* on which I've been lucky enough to interview some legendary names, from George Foreman to Joe Namath to Al Leiter. But since the focus is gambling, I try to have the biggest names in the world of wagering.

Degenerate gamblers like Artie Lange come on and tell great stories, as did World Series of Poker champion Phil Hellmuth and Molly Bloom, the woman who ran the biggest underground poker games in the world.

But for the longest time I was unable to nab the gold-standard guest when it comes to a cross between sports and gambling: baseball's hit leader Pete Rose.

For those of you not familiar with Pete's story, despite posting the greatest numbers imaginable for a major-league hitter, Pete Rose was banned from baseball when it was revealed that he had bet on games while he was managing the Reds.

It's also worth mentioning that he sucked at it. Rose would lose tens of thousands of dollars over the course of a week, which is pretty much all you need to know about sports gambling. One of the highest baseball IQs in history couldn't figure out how to make a buck wagering on it. I actually think this should have been a mitigating factor in the decision to ban him, but, unfortunately for Pete, I have nothing to do with those decrees. Every commissioner since Peter Ueberroth has either denied Pete Rose's bid for reinstatement and access to the Hall of Fame or, worse yet, ignored it.

So Pete did the honorable thing. He set up a booth in the Caesars Palace Forum shops in Las Vegas and signed autographs. Making a living inside a casino is maybe not the best way to prove that you have gambling out of your system, but, hey, I don't begrudge the guy for trying to make a few bucks. Pete Rose has probably signed more autographs than anyone in American history. And I'm including any doctor who has carelessly scribbled a prescription for Z packs.

I tried to get Pete Rose on my podcast several times, to no avail. It never worked out. His representation always said he wanted money or the timing wasn't right. Then, in the summer of 2019, my friend Andy approached me with the opportunity I had been waiting for. Andy is Tony Romo's mother's sister's son. I met him about a decade ago and immediately took a liking to him, mainly for his passion for sports and gambling but also for being the cousin of a famous person. It's a fun fraternity that includes me, Andy, and Chachi from *Happy Days*.

Anyway, Andy was starting up the first-ever SportsCon, which is similar to Comic-Con except with athletes and not comic book heroes. And unlike Comic-Con, most of the patrons have gotten to second base with a woman.

Cousin Andy footed the bill for a hundred athletes/sports personalities to appear. I insisted he didn't pay me. I told him I'd let him put a picture of my fat head in the brochure if he could get me twenty minutes with Pete Rose. I'd sign autographs. Host dumb games. Let bratty kids throw pie in my face...whatever he wanted. The fact that I had done 130 episodes of a sports gambling podcast and not one of them featured Pete Rose was ridiculous.

Cousin Andy agreed to make it work. I flew the family out to Dallas and set us up at the Marriott, which was a two-minute walk from the site where JFK was (allegedly?) assassinated. Probably a sign as to how the weekend was going to turn out.

When I got to the venue, I locked eyes with Pete. He was wearing a pink cap with matching collar and cuffs. He dressed like he wanted to be in public but his body language suggested otherwise. Now in his late seventies, Pete walked in the same crouched stance he used to bang out an opposite-field single. Cousin Andy introduced me to Rose, and just as I was about to start my recording device, Andy whispered to me, "He doesn't know this is a gambling podcast so maybe don't mention *Against All Odds*."

Great. I was already starting the interview with a called strike. But Rose had briefly written about gambling in the book he was promoting, so maybe it wouldn't be a problem.

I introduced myself and told Pete I had been wanting to talk to him for a long time and that I had flown all the way to Dallas just to interview him. He looked at me as if I had just explained that I had found a dime while walking on Hollywood Boulevard. Not very impressed. Swing and a miss—strike two.

I got some mojo back as the interview progressed by recounting his amazing stats, talked about what an influence he was on other great hitters, how proud his father must have been—everything he wanted to hear. Still, Pete Rose is the kind of guy who agrees with everything you say but is still angry that you're making sense. He's basically Pete Rose.

At about the twenty-minute mark of this ass kissing, Rose's handler started to hover. He approached with three dozen baseballs for him to sign, an indication that the end of the interview was near.

Was I really not going to ask him...no, I WAS going to ask him about gambling. I would have no respect for myself as a journalist or whatever the hell I am if I hadn't. I took the Lieutenant Kaffee deep breath and nervous sip of water before interrogating Colonel Jessup.

> **Me:** I know you don't love discussing this, but I want to talk about the gambling stuff for a second.

Pete rears back in as defensive a posture as I've ever seen on a human being.

> **Me:** I read your book and you remember everything. You knew dates that no one else would care about. You knew your batting average with three weeks left in the 1960 season back when you played class D minor league-ball for Geneva. I think what happened was you were a numbers guy and you got bored managing and you decided—
>
> **Pete:** I was bored and I screwed up.
>
> **Me:** Right. But baseball is a game of second chances. Don't you think if you would've come clean and said that you didn't bet against your team that they would've cut you some slack?
>
> **Pete:** Listen. This happened in 1989. What's that...thirty years ago? Do you really think your listeners want to hear about this thirty years later?

Me: I actually think they would…

Pete: Like I said, I screwed up. I moved on. And you need to move on to another question…WHICH WILL BE YOUR LAST QUESTION!!

Asshole. I'm actually taking his side and, yes, listeners of a sports gambling podcast would most certainly want to hear whether the guy who is not in the Hall of Fame wagered against his own team. This reminded me of when Monica Lewinsky came on *Jimmy Kimmel Live!* and refused to discuss anything related to her time in the White House.

I was allowed one more question, so I had to dig deep into my bag of nonsensical queries.

Me: One more question?

Pete: Yep.

Me: Do you think you and I will hang out anytime soon?

And that was that. After dropping the mic, Charlie hustled his ass out of the interview.

In retrospect, had I known he was going to be an even bigger dick than I imagined, I would've asked him something more gambling-centric, like: "If you're holding on to a six-team parlay that pays 30/1 with five winners in, how much do you hedge on the sixth game?"

Following his departure, I actually started to feel bad for Pete. His publicist didn't tell him he was sitting down to talk about sports gambling. In his mind it was an ambush. Whatever. Maybe I wouldn't post the interview I had waited so very long to get.

It was then that I made arrangements to meet up with my

family at the opposite end of the venue, about a ten-minute walk away. We were going to meet up at the makeshift batting cage. I got sidetracked when a couple of Kimmel fans miraculously recognized me and asked to take selfies.

When I finally caught up to the rest of the family, my five-year-old son, Harrison, was about to hit off a tee, and who is sitting next to him on a stool? Pete Motherfucking Rose. I had the presence of mind to start recording on my phone. I need to brag a little here. Harrison was the best baseball player on his team and hadn't hit off a tee since he was three, so I could tell he was going to be distracted by a baseball on a stick.

Sure enough, Harrison goes after it with all of his thirty-five-pound might and clobbers the middle of the tee. The ball slowly dribbles off to the ground. And then the three words any little boy would love to hear from a strange, bitter old man.

Pete: Take a hike.

I posted this five-second video on Twitter with the caption: "Here's Pete telling my five-year-old to take a hike. I guess Pete had money on him hitting a triple."

It got over 500,000 views. I couldn't be happier. Now a half a million people know he's a sullen schmuck.

As far as I was concerned, that was Pete Rose's third strike with me, so I was going to post the interview.

Most important, I can rest easy knowing that, despite the fact that my son Harrison whiffed on the tee, he has a better chance of getting into the Hall of Fame than Pete Rose.

HARRY HARRY HIPPO

It's interesting to see what motivates people to change their lifestyles. Often they're driven by stern talks from their primary physicians, who will outline the next few years of their lives if they don't strive for a healthier existence. In my friend Harry's case that talk off the ledge came in the form of a few thousand dollars and the promise of not being naked in front of a crowd.

Harry was very thin when I met him in college. He probably weighed 135 pounds soaking wet with Labatt Blue. Don't get me wrong: he was still a very odd-looking nineteen-year-old, but as far as girth went, he weighed less than the stack of scratch-off lottery tickets he disposed of weekly.

Genetics caught up with him, and within a few short years he was, as David Letterman called Atlanta Braves pitcher Terry Forster, "a big fat tub of goo."

So, in March of 2017, for Harry's well-being and, more important, for the good of my gambling podcast, I proposed a bet. My proposition went like this: if Harry could lose fifty-two pounds before Super Bowl 52, I would pay him $5,200. If he fell short of that goal, he would be forced to stand on Hollywood Boulevard wearing nothing but his underwear and a sandwich board that read "I'M HARRY HARRY HIPPO THE FAT LOSER WHO COULDN'T LOSE FAT." He'd have to do this all day long while singing Daughtry songs very loudly.

I thought this was a fair trade-off. A complete lifestyle change and, if he didn't make it, a full day of embarrassment. The Daughtry part wouldn't be deemed as embarrassing by Harry, who was weirdly infatuated with the *American Idol* season 5 fourth-place finisher. The nude part took some convincing, but I reminded Harry that Hollywood Boulevard was such a freak zone that he wouldn't be a blip on the tourists' radar. It was a lie, but I had to get him to agree.

So this was going to happen. A few days after the bet was proposed, Harry weighed himself at a local veterinarian's office in Phoenix where his boss and our friend Ken forced him to take his dogs every week despite the fact that there was never anything wrong with them.

The poor scale screamed 246.8. Pretty high for Harry, who is not particularly tall. Height-wise he's somewhere between a full-grown panda and a half-grown Yao Ming. That made 194.8 the target goal, or 52 pounds in ten months. This was going to be tough sledding for Harry, who had a number of factors stacked against him. For one, he lives with Ken, who routinely orders pizza at 9:30 p.m. and makes you feel like an asshole if, after he eats five slices, you don't finish off the remaining three.

Also, he resides in Phoenix, where outdoor exercising is limited during the 119-degree summer months. Always thinking,

I insisted on a clause that read if Harry were to die, he would automatically lose the bet. We'd prop him up against the wall like *Weekend at Bernie's* with a sandwich board and that would be that. The singing part would have to be figured out, but everything else was in place.

Finally, he's Harry. He'd become very accustomed to snuggling up to a sleeve of Pringles in the middle of the night while watching South Korean golf tournaments that he had bet on.

But something took over. A force more powerful than Snap, Crackle, and Pop combined. Harry took control of his life. He cut out carbs. He ignored Ken's caloric temptations.

He began running in place in his pool for hours on end while listening to Daughtry. He played tennis against a wall. He hiked mountains in the greater Paradise Valley area.

Harry was losing the weight at a steady pace. Every Tuesday topless Harry would jump on the vet's scale and shoot a quick inspirational video. I'm sure it also inspired the workers at the animal hospital to find new employment.

Every week he'd report a lower number. By the end of the regular season, it was looking good for him to cash in on this bet.

In an effort to solidify the win, a few days before the Super Bowl, Harry gave himself a mineral oil enema. The fact that he stooped so low as to shoot lubricants into his anus pretty much meant I'd won the bet, regardless of the financial outcome.

In a last-ditch attempt to get Harry to cave, on Super Bowl Eve I took him and a few friends to a steak house and ordered just about everything on the menu. What was an extra couple hundred bucks if I stood to lose over $5K? We all ate like we were going to be lethally injected postmeal…except for Harry.

He toughed it out for two hours consuming nothing but an ice water with lemon.

It didn't look promising for me. Harry was committed. He had me beat. It was a formality at this point. The morning of the big game we drove to a Super Bowl party. On hand for the epic moment were the former hosts of *The Man Show*—Adam Carolla and my cousin Jimmy Kimmel—and a bunch of confused children.

So now it was time. Harry stepped up to the scale wearing crimson underwear that appeared to have been passed down from ancestors who had served in the Civil War. He had about four pounds of unshaved chest hair, which signaled that he was as confident as he had ever been. He walked up to a standard human scale. Stepped on with both feet...

The scale read 191.8 pounds. Harry made it with a full three pounds to spare. I was actually proud of him. It showed tremendous commitment and was easily the greatest accomplishment of his life. I handed the money right over and he immediately handed $150 over to my friend Kevin's daughter, who was peddling Girl Scout cookies. He was about to Thin Mint his way back to fat city.

I told my cousin Jimmy that, just for the fun of it, I was going to rebound by betting Harry $5,300 that he couldn't gain 53 pounds by Super Bowl 53. Jimmy advised me to not offer Harry any cash incentive but rather to just sit back and watch it happen naturally. And, sure as shit, it did. Take a look at the pictures. The proof is in the tapioca pudding. There is no denying the human spirit.

AND THE WINNER IS...NOT ME

Some of the most exciting sports bets are those that are so close they are left up to judges to decide. Whether you're waiting for a decision to be announced in a boxing match or an ice skating compulsory, it can be pretty intense to know that a screaming man in a bow tie or a Bulgarian former Olympian is about to determine your financial fate.

A similar phenomenon takes place when you wager on awards shows, only in this case, the presenter, maybe in the form of Helen Mirren in a floor-length embroidered floral gown, is breaking the news, good or bad. It still comes down to a single reveal of a decision that is completely out of your hands. And then in your hands. And then back out again. Hang in there. This is a good one.

I've been fortunate enough to write for my cousin Jimmy when he hosted two Emmys and two Academy Awards shows.

Without sounding like a sap, I maintain that, as stuffy as the crowd may seem on TV, the electricity fueled by the buildup and passion for the Oscars is second to none. The first time Jimmy hosted the Oscars was the funnest and most professionally rewarding night of my and my cowriters' lives. His monologue crushed, and besides that, we had some very solid live bits planned.

We dropped various candies from the ceiling of the Dolby Theatre in order to feed a bunch of A-listers who hadn't eaten in five hours, and in some cases five months to fit into their dresses. A cutaway of Meryl Streep victoriously clutching a box of Junior Mints made the whole thing worthwhile.

We also commandeered a bus full of unwitting tourists and led them into the studio. Everyone on the tour got to meet celebrities sitting in the front row as Jimmy ushered them from one side of the arena to the other. The star of that ambush was "Gary from Chicago," who became an instant Internet sensation. There were reports that we'd staged the tour bus prank, but those reports were debunked when a few days later it was revealed that Gary from Chicago had been out of jail just three days after serving twenty years for, among other things, attempted rape. You can't ever win with these things.

Gary from Chicago's past aside, this was still the coolest night imaginable. I was so happy for Jimmy, who killed.

So why did I have to sully it with a wager? Because that's the kind of thing I do. Luckily my bookie, Lloyd, is just as nuts. He lets me bet on anything. This particular evening I had three winners for my Oscar parlay. I already won with Casey Affleck for best actor, Mahershala Ali for best supporting actor, and Viola Davis for best supporting actress. All I needed was for La La Land, a 1/3 favorite, to win Best Picture.

La La Land told the story of an aspiring actress and a

dedicated jazz musician struggling to make ends meet in a city known for crushing hopes and breaking hearts. That's my capsule summary of *La La Land*. Or maybe I lifted that from Rotten Tomatoes. The point is it was a celebration of Hollywood that people in Hollywood love.

It had also already won the Golden Globe and a BAFTA award. Two great indicators as to how a movie is going to do at the Oscars. In my mind, I had this locked up.

So there we were: three hours and forty-five minutes into the telecast. Hollywood legends Warren Beatty and Faye Dunaway were presenting the final award. They walked out and neither looked like they particularly wanted to be there. A few minutes later they would wish they had never been born. They went through the nominees and then it was time to announce a winner. Warren looked at the envelope and handed it to Faye, who uttered the words *"La La Land."*

The cast got onstage to celebrate, and all of a sudden...bedlam.

Backstage, I was just done high-fiving myself for the big win, when I heard "No! No! No!"

Fat guys with mullets and headsets were scrambling...Did they all have spontaneous diarrhea? Were we being attacked by terrorists?

One of the frantic producers made his way to the stage, interrupting acceptance speeches. He grabbed the microphone and said, "I'm sorry. There's been a mistake. *Moonlight*...you guys won Best Picture."

Okay, it wasn't a terrorist attack. But now we had to figure out if we were being punked by some guy in a tuxedo pretending to be a producer. That wasn't the case.

The *Moonlight* producers then sidled up to the stage to deliver their acceptance speeches. My cousin Jimmy, who was now sitting in the front row with his mortal enemy, Matt Damon, jumped up. It was his duty to sign off and close the show.

Jimmy said, "This is very unfortunate. Personally I blame Steve Harvey for this" (referring to Steve Harvey's gaffe at the Miss Universe competition). Jimmy fittingly got the final laugh of the evening.

But everyone was still confused. This was going to be a huge deal. Not the part where I suffered a $3,500 swing on my Oscar parlay. The fact that someone read the wrong name or was given the wrong envelope or something. How in the effing crap was this possible?

Turned out some douchebag accountant from PricewaterhouseCoopers was distracted taking selfies with stars and mistakenly gave Faye and Warren the wrong envelope—the one that named Emma Stone as Best Actress for her role in *La La Land*. Dunaway just saw "*La La Land*," hence the reason those words came out of her mouth.

In a lot of ways it was the worst beat I've ever suffered in that I WAS ALREADY DECLARED A WINNER.

Ryan Gosling and Emma Stone were so gracious. Every one of my cowriters was celebrating a job well done. It was a big load off and now they got to party. And then there was me, throwing a tantrum in the bowels of the Dolby Theatre.

There was no Oscar for acting coming my way that night. I don't drink, so drowning my sorrows wasn't an option, but you could bet I would overdose on pretzel bread at the Governor's Ball.

You might say that's what you get for betting on an awards show...but then, you don't really get it. Or maybe *I* don't really get it. Please enjoy more examples of me not getting it.

THE WORLDWIDE LEADER IN PICKS

In the spring of 2014 I got a call from my agent at the time, James "Baby Doll" Dixon. I'm still with him, but I say "at the time" because Baby Doll now claims he's a manager to avoid problems with the Writers Guild. Long story, but I thought this was as good a spot as any to out him on that.

Anyway, Baby Doll relayed a message saying ESPN had hired me for an NFL picks segment on *SportsCenter* starting in September. This was a great thrill and, at the same time, a head-scratcher. The Worldwide Leader in Sports wanted to hire me—the World Wide Leader in Losing Parlays—to pick games in front of their massive audience. As a professional degenerate gambler, it didn't get much better than this.

Baby Doll's call didn't come out of nowhere, as I had auditioned for this job against a couple other folks a month before. These other candidates knew a lot more about sports gambling nuances than I did. The problem is, many of these statistical geniuses aren't TV-ready. They're great with numbers, but when the lights are turned on, most of them look like they're shooting a hostage video. I'm no Jude Law on the small screen, either, but if all else looks-wise fails—and let's face it, it pretty much has—a personality goes a long way.

It also helps to be paired with professional broadcasters who make it look seamless. Kenny Mayne, Neil Everett, and Stan Verrett fit this bill to a T.

Stan's a nice guy—not as interested in gambling as the others—but a football junkie, nonetheless. Don't get him started on Louisiana sports. Say something derogatory about Drew Brees and he'll reach into his lapel and smack you with a beignet.

I have known Kenny Mayne for over a decade. In my estimation he's on the Mount Rushmore of ESPN anchors. Truth be told, I have, like, eight dudes on my ESPN Mount Rushmore. It's too hard to choose; I don't know how they figured out the one with the presidents. Kenny and I played various celebrity softball games together. He'd bat cleanup. I'd bat fifteenth. He likes to bet horses, too. Every now and then, I still get a text from Kenny with seventeen different horse numbers. Then afterward: "Well, how much did you win?" I never know what to do with them, so I usually just tell him I screwed up and parlayed the wrong ones.

Neil Everett was my guy. About 90 percent of my segments were with Neil. He had some experience betting on pro football and did everything in his power not to let me pull him back into the vortex of vig. Neil would risk a few dollars back in the day, and did it while living in Hawaii, which sounded insane. The Sunday games kick off at 7:00 a.m. on the islands. Neil once told me how hard it was, living in Hawaii, to hide the fact you have a gambling problem from your roommate. "Why else would anyone be screaming at a TV at 7:00 a.m. on a Sunday? Everyone on the island is so chill, and you're losing your mind because Billy Joe Tolliver threw his third pick in the first quarter."

Neil went along with all of my shenanigans. I would typically pick a game I thought was fishy, then take an underdog, and finish off with my best bet, followed by a quick comedic moment. These moments often involved poking fun at Neil's chest hair. Every week I'd have a crazy Ralph Kramden–esque harebrained scheme. I'd walk up to him as he was writing copy for the 11:00 p.m. *SportsCenter*. "Neil, would you mind slapping me in the face with a football covered with shaving cream? Don't ask. I promise it will make sense." He never questioned this. So easygoing.

I'm not sure everyone else at ESPN was as confident in my staying power early on. I remember asking the segment producer for a bunch of parking validations so that I didn't have to bother him every week. He replied, "How about I give you one after each segment?" What a vote of confidence!

But then, a miracle occurred. I started winning. I was somehow very successful during my tenure at ESPN. Like, off-the-charts successful. Look it up. In 2014–2015 I went 15-0-3 over the last six regular season weeks. Eighteen bets in a row without a loss. And the best part: I didn't make a dime off of the bets. I was too superstitious and felt, if I bet them myself, they would go down the shitter. In fact, I actually lost money during my hot streak. As my degenerate buddies who typically lose would jump on my picks and, knowing they were hard to collect from, would just book them myself.

ESPN renewed me for season two, and guess what? I remained on fire: 13-3-1 with my best bets. I was hitting games at a 75 percent clip over two seasons. Anyone can get lucky over a short time, but two years? I was starting to believe my own bullshit. My documented run was really nothing like anything that had been seen on television before.

I was so prolific that a Yahoo! sportswriter by the name of Cork Gaines wrote an article praising my picks. I should've been happy, but I was actually confused and a little bummed out. I arranged for a meeting with my boss at ESPN, the guy responsible for *SportsCenter*.

I had some complaints. My segment was buried deep on ESPN.com, underneath Australian Rules football—a sport the network hadn't aired in twenty-five years. Meanwhile, they were getting scooped by Yahoo! sports, which, every way you looked at it, was ESPN's competition.

He told me to shut the door and sit down. Somehow I had a feeling I wasn't about to get a retroactive ESPY award. He started saying things like "We can't celebrate your success too much here" and "We have to do this thing tongue in cheek." He further explained that not everyone in the organization was as stoked about giving out gambling picks as I was. He told me that ESPN pays $2 billion for the Monday night game and that they didn't want to rock the boat with a commissioner who, at the time, if he had his choice, would've rounded up everyone who as much as strolled by a Las Vegas sportsbook and sent them off to Guantánamo Bay.

I countered by pointing out that the NFL gives ESPN one of the shittiest games to air each week. How much worse could they make things?

But I wasn't getting anywhere. It was what it was, and it wasn't about me. They were only willing to dip their toe in the gambling cesspool and pretend to be interested. At least, that's how bitter old me looked at it.

Whatever. I did the best I could to provide an entertaining sports gambling segment. That's all I could do. I prepared for season 3 but hadn't heard from the producer I had normally dealt with. Things were weird until Baby Doll finally called me and broke the news: I had been fired... or, to put it nicely, my segment had not been picked up.

The explanation they gave Baby Doll was that they liked me a lot but had to cut costs. I was the latest casualty in the ESPN round of firings.

I picked games at a 75 percent rate and was fired from their gambling segment.

This was akin to if the guy who had been rewarded for killing Osama bin Laden were dishonorably discharged by the Navy SEALs.

Yes, I am equating my guessing which team will cover the spread to eradicating one of the most evil villains ever to walk planet Earth.

The point is it didn't make any sense, but it didn't have to. I had a job writing and performing on *Jimmy Kimmel Live!*, so my family wasn't going to starve, but it still sucked.

What could I do with this incredible gift?

I thought about selling picks like the guys who would bug me in college, but then came to the realization that it was too scummy. You need a hard-core salesman to upsell gambling packages. Not to mention, I would receive near death threats for my losing picks when they were free. If I was charging people and the picks were bad, I could wash up somewhere near the Santa Monica pier.

I brought the news of my firing to my cousin Jimmy. He barely looked up from his laptop—which is a good thing, because I don't think the tears in my eyes had dried—and presented me with an idea for the fall. He had met this guy Rob at a poker tournament. Rob was a savant who had family connections at the top of the Facebook food chain. He was a master at manipulating the algorithm ensuring the maximum amount of viewers for a given post. He would use sponsor money to buy what are called "impressions," which would guarantee my video would end up on someone's feed as long as they listed football and gambling in their "likes." It's a fascinating process and we tested it out on a Facebook show we called *Cousin Sal's Sure Thing*.

The show would consist of three parts: a Friday picks segment, a Sunday live check-in, and a recap on Tuesday.

The recaps had to be done without logos or highlights so as to not freak the league out. This led to some creative editing featuring actual African lions thrashing actual half-eaten bottlenose dolphins around in their mouths and similar hardcore stock footage from nature shows.

The Friday picks were done in front of a green screen of the Caesars Palace sportsbook. It was made to look like I was in Las Vegas even though in reality I was shooting from a sixty-four-square-foot pantry in Santa Monica. For one of the segments I was able to wrangle Johnny Knoxville to punch me in the nuts after a losing bet. He was a true gentleman for doing it.

But the Sunday check-in was the highlight of *Cousin Sal's Sure Thing*. The plan was to sign onto Facebook Live in between the early and late afternoon games, talking about my bad beats and discussing the gambling implications for each early game.

For the Facebook Live hit, I'd go on with my buddy Scott. Scott was a Longhorns fan from Texas who would bemoan Cowboys losses with me while downing pilsners. That was really his only purpose. And then there was Brad, who would get to the warehouse at 10:00 a.m. with a bag full of candy and a six-pack of Orange Crush soda. Eventually these goodies took their toll and Brad would pass out from 11:30 a.m. until about thirty-five seconds before we went on live.

It was problematic to be talking football when Brad was stuck in a Kit Kat coma. One week we tricked him and said that Tom Brady was out for the year after Bill Belichick kept him in for a meaningless play down the stretch. Having slept through the fourth quarter, Brad took our word for it and started to defend the Patriots coach. "This is the Patriots' way. They don't take their foot off the gas. He's going to take a lot of shit for this, but that's how they operate." Scott and I looked at him and started laughing. He knew immediately he had been set up. He hit us with a "Very clever" and then went back to sleep.

As far as the picks went, I struggled to stay above 50 percent. The ESPN magic was gone and, after half the season, so was our sponsor. I won't mention who they were for fear that someone will use their shitty razors and bleed out over their sink.

The bottom line is that they, like everyone else, got cold feet when it came to the gambling stuff. This is how it was. I was always going to be seen as an outcast by the TV networks and sponsors.

And thank the gambling gods and Jesus Christ himself the Supreme Court changed all that...

HAIL TO THE CHIEFS (-5.5)

Politics suck and I, for the most part, want nothing to do with it. Especially at the national level. I am much more pissed off about a pothole that's not fixed than whether or not some blowhard is golfing too much on the job.

I don't want to get preachy, but the truth is, while many presidential candidates have good intentions, if they get elected and try to keep the promises they ran on, they find themselves handcuffed by Congress and are unable to see their visions through. Nothing ever gets done, so why pretend that the man or woman you vote for is going to make a difference?

I know this is an irresponsible way to look at things, but add it to the list of irresponsible things I stand for. I'm just not interested in politics. In fact, in order to generate interest, I'll gamble on—you guessed it—the presidential race.

I more or less got started gambling on presidential elections at the age of thirteen, half a decade before I was even allowed to vote. My social studies teacher, Mr. Gieg, was a real character. I enjoyed him as much as anyone can enjoy a man in his mid-forties who still had braces. He made learning fun, and when the 1984 election rolled around, he set up a competition. Everyone in the class had to guess the final electoral vote tally. Whoever was closest to the correct total would receive a $10 gift card to Modell's Sporting Goods. Despite having the gambling bug, I really had a desire to purchase a New York Islanders Stanley Cup pennant, so I became very focused on figuring out how to win this thing.

The incumbent, Ronald Reagan, was expected to crush Walter Mondale, so I was going with a big number. Back then there was no Situation Room or online predictor apps, so I had to take matters into my own hands. I studied the results of previous elections, read up on swing states, and asked other adults who seemed to know what they were talking about and finally came up with 519. It was an excellent guess and would've been enough to cash in on the gift card if Robert Marsh hadn't guessed 525, which was THE EXACT EFFING NUMBER. How was that even possible? I mean, this was Biff Tannen *Back to the Future Part II*–type shit.

Fast-forward thirty-two years, when I would suffer an even worse political bad beat during a low-key, quiet presidential election involving Hillary Clinton and Donald Trump. I was all over Hillary like white on Condoleezza Rice. (I acknowledge that doesn't make sense, but it sounds good.)

I laid $4 to win $1 that Hillary would win the election...but by many, many, many multiples of that ratio. And that wasn't all. I also loaded up on Hillary to win battleground states such as Michigan, Pennsylvania, Florida, and Wisconsin. I bet them all individually and paid a hefty price for each one. And they all lost by the slimmest of margins, leading to my incurring the fattest of debts.

Call me crazy, but I just couldn't see the guy who, a few weeks earlier, was busted on tape bragging about grabbing vaginas having access to the nuclear football. But it happened, and so, on November 8, 2016, whatever money I was theoretically getting back in taxes from the Republicans was squandered tenfold.

I didn't hate Trump nearly as much as everyone rooting against him did. In fact, I had met him a few months before and we had a perfectly fine exchange. The Donald appeared on my cousin Jimmy Kimmel's late-night show. At that time there were, like, seven Republican hopefuls, so I, as a gag, put on the red hat and headed down to the greenroom with two other writers who were also tickled by the idea of meeting the *Celebrity Apprentice* dude who was about to come in seventh place for the losing party.

Trump came out of his dressing room immediately. He approached us and used his tiny hand to shake ours.

> **Me:** It's nice to have you here.
>
> **Trump:** I'm excited to be here. I love Jimmy. You guys are writers? How many writers do you have?
>
> **Me:** We have thirteen writers. Fourteen if we include you.
>
> **Trump:** Oh, right, I'm responsible for a lot of material, aren't I?
>
> **Me:** Yes—you are. Keep up the good work.

Pretty uneventful and not nearly as remarkable as a few years before, when I met President Obama.

My cousin Jimmy was given the once-in-a-lifetime, super-cool gig of roasting the president at the White House Correspondents' Association dinner. In my totally biased opinion, he did a terrific job.

He did an even better job coordinating his entourage. Jimmy traveled to DC with fourteen friends/relatives/publicists/agents. He made P Diddy look like a loner. I was lucky and related enough to be asked to be one of Jay-K's "pluses."

We were told that we might get to meet the president and his wife. All week I thought, *What am I going to say to him? I'll probably have about twenty seconds.* Enough time to tell him what an honor it was to shake his hand and to take a picture with a few seconds to spare.

Then came the big night. About an hour before the dinner, Jimmy's companions were escorted across the Hilton Hotel through a comical maze of security stops. It was the equivalent of walking through fifteen airports at once without a whiff of Cinnabon.

Finally, after several important people told us we were not supposed to be wherever we were, our group was led into a room full of friends and relatives of everyone appearing on the dais or about to receive an award that night. About seventy-five people total. We were told that the president and Mrs. Obama would be joining us in a half hour. We'd have one shot at a picture, either alone or in a large or small group.

My friend Daniel, whose claim to fame as a producer was convincing Drew Barrymore during her 1995 *Late Night* appearance to flash David Letterman on his birthday, attempted to choreograph my encounter,

Daniel: Why don't you take your picture with Baby Doll and tell Obama that he didn't vote for him?

I've already spoken about my tough-talking, chain-smoking agent, James "Baby Doll" Dixon. At this point it's well established that he's likely my biggest prank target on the planet.

Years ago, while driving through Atlanta, when Baby Doll was bragging to a bunch of ABC affiliates about how expensive his sunglasses were, I took the glasses right off his face and tossed them out the sunroof.

Once we were at an early-morning big meeting where a soda company attempted to woo my cousin Jimmy and convince him to become their next spokesman. Baby Doll had been up late, and as he started to nod off, I chucked a plastic bottle cap from long range and hit him directly in the forehead. He called me a dick in front of a dozen suits as they stopped their PowerPoint presentation to witness the ensuing ridiculous back-and-forth.

After each of these, and countless other scenarios, Baby Doll gave me a Joe Pesci/*Goodfellas*-esque tongue-lashing, only to forgive me later on.

So you can see that convincing Baby Doll to forfeit his solo picture with the Obamas to take one with me was going to be a tall order. But I had to give it a try.

I knew if I convinced him and he had time to think about it, he would change his mind, so I waited until we were about third in line to meet the Obamas. I sidled up to Baby Doll and, utilizing my most deadpan hidden-camera acting abilities:

Me: Baby—can I be honest with you?
Baby Doll: Sure, Baby Doll. What is it?

Me: It would be an honor for me to take a picture with
you and the president.

Baby Doll: Fuck that, Baby, I'm not wasting the picture.
You're just gonna do something stupid.

Me: No, Baby, really. I would love nothing more than to
have a picture of us and the president on my mantel.

Baby Doll: Why, Baby? Why can't you just take one
alone?

Me: It would just mean a lot.

Baby Doll (hesitating): All right, Baby Doll, if it means
that much to you. But no fucking around.

Me: Of course not. This is the president.

Way easier than I thought. I must've caught him during
a weak moment. Just a day earlier, during the White House
tour, I had shoved him into the Rose Garden, for God's sake.
(Really, I did.)

What the hell was he thinking? *Who cares* what he was
thinking?

The truth was I hadn't voted for Obama, while Baby Doll
had. But no one needed to know that. I was all set. Then came
our turn...

Me: Hello, Mr. President. Sal Iacono. It's an honor to
meet you.

President Obama: Very nice to meet you, Sal.

I repeat a similar intro to First Lady Michelle Obama. Baby
Doll does the same to both.

Me (to President Obama): I want you to know I voted for you, but my friend Baby Doll over here didn't.

We take the picture.

President Obama (to Baby Doll): Well, you still have one more chance.

Michelle (to Baby Doll): Yes, you still have one more chance.

Baby Doll (startled, having not heard what I said originally): Excuse me?

Everyone is now staring at everyone else.

Baby Doll (now realizing what has happened): Oh, don't listen to this guy, Mr. President. I was the first one in my district at the polling...

Me (ushering Baby Doll away from the Obamas): You heard them, Baby: you still have one more chance. Let's leave these people alone now. They're very busy.

And that was that. Baby and I walked away bickering about nonsense as the president and Mrs. Obama looked on, amused and confused. Mostly confused.

I have to give Baby Doll credit. It took every nicotine-stained fiber of his being to not use the F-word or call me a dick in front of the president and his wife.

In retrospect, I really wish he had.

MOUNT ODDSMORE

Every few weeks on my *Against All Odds* podcast my Degenerate Trifecta and I allow listeners to present their cases via email asking whether or not they belong in my fictitious Degenerate Gamblers Hall of Fame. The four of us vote and, if three give the nod, the listener gets a bust in our make-believe shrine in Pahrump, Nevada. There's nothing to see, because, as I tell the listeners, the facility is under construction. Also, it doesn't exist.

We hear all kinds of things. Listeners who have won bets as a result of marrying somebody they didn't like. Even a man who died in a sauna contest was given a posthumous welcome into our fake institution. Whether the Degenerate Gamblers Hall of Fame exists or not, there's no denying that legendary bettors need to be memorialized for their contributions to the casinos' bottom line.

It's always tough to put together a Mount Rushmore of anything. Narrowing pro wrestlers, NBA players, one-hit-wonder musicians, teamsters, or even movies about dogs down to four legends is a near-impossible task. Did you know the original Mount Rushmore was supposed to comprise ten presidents, but the awl broke and the guy doing the chiseling was, like, "Fuck it, we end on Lincoln"?

Still, I find it necessary to put together a Mount Oddsmore, if you will. I'm sure the history books are riddled with fabled card counters, incredibly wealthy and ballsy Asian men, or old-timey lords who were beheaded three hundred years ago, but I'm going to go with the four that I feel have impacted their ecosystem the most.

JIMMY "THE GREEK" SNYDER

A slovenly man picking NFL games on TV? That's me in a do-nut shell. Why wouldn't I put him on Mount Oddsmore? Jimmy "the Greek" Snyder was about thirty-five years before his time. Of course, in the 1980s, when networks and the league weren't so keen on betting on NFL games, he was never able to mention the spread on national television, but he would often signal with his hands "small" or "big" to communicate whether a team was going to cover the actual spread. His appearances on CBS pregame shows were highlighted by behind-the-scenes battles with Brent Musburger, a quiet degenerate who Jimmy was once rumored to have punched in the face at a bar.

The Greek started this glorious run befriending local book-makers at a very young age in Steubenville, Ohio. Legend has it that, in 1948 he received a tip and bet $10,000 on Harry Truman at 17/1 odds, which would have paid him $170,000. There's no telling how he came across this money or who took this wager or if it was ever paid out, but who cares? It's an epic tale and we're going with it.

The Greek moved to Vegas in the mid-1950s, where he started making book. The fact that he was able to stay out of jail was enough to eventually land him a CBS pregame gig. The Greek had a great gimmick and was loved by all until making some drunken racially charged statements and that was that. CBS had to let him go.

According to the ESPN *30 for 30* documentary, a penniless Snyder died of a heart attack in Las Vegas, a demise I would give even odds that I will share.

BILLY WALTERS

The legendary Billy Walters was similar to Jimmy in that he tried desperately to get an edge on the sports gambling industry, but, unlike the Greek, Walters did whatever he could to stay out of the public eye. In doing so, Billy Walters is widely known as the most successful sports gambler in Las Vegas, with a winning record spanning three decades.

Walters started off a loser like the rest of us. Even worse. He was said to have dropped $1 million playing blackjack in Las Vegas. Twice. But then he and his friends got smart. He noticed a flaw in a roulette wheel and bet the same numbers over and over until he won nearly $40 million in just over thirty-five hours. That's a solid hourly wage.

Shortly after, Walters put together a consortium that used computer analysis to predict sports outcomes. The computer enabled him to win every year for thirty-nine years except for one. Those of us who can't put together two winning Sundays in a row know that thirty-eight out of thirty-nine winning years is an insane accomplishment.

Of course, everything good has to come to an end, and Billy Walters is currently serving five years at the Federal Prison Camp Pensacola for insider trading. When he gets out, he'll have the privilege of seeing his likeness on Mount Oddsmore.

AMARILLO SLIM

Mount Oddsmore would not be complete without a poker player. It would be like putting together a list of the four best Girl Scout cookies and not including Samoas. (Don't get me started on this one: Samoas win hands down.) Anyway, I could've gone with Phil Ivey, Daniel Negreanu, Phil Hellmuth, or one of the giants at the top of the all-time poker leaderboard.

I might've dipped into *Back to the Future Part III* territory and picked Wild Bill Hickok, a notorious gambler from the Wild Wild West who was shot in the head while playing five-card stud. At the time he was supposedly holding pairs of aces and eights, which is now known as "the dead man's hand."

But, in the end, I decided to split the difference and go with another plucky poker pioneer named Thomas Preston Jr., aka Amarillo Slim. First off, will we ever come up with a better nickname for a poker player or anyone? Amarillo Slim is right up there with Marvelous Marvin Hagler, Magic Johnson, and He Hate Me as one of the greatest monikers in sports/entertainment history.

Slim had the grit factor going for him, competing in back-room games where you were more likely to get stabbed than paid. He won the World Series of Poker back in 1972, a total of four World Series of Poker bracelets. Slim reportedly played against Presidents Lyndon Johnson and Richard Nixon as well as the famed international president of drugs, Pablo Escobar.

But it was the ultra-creative prop bets invented by Amarillo Slim that put him over the top for me. He rarely ever lost one, and all of his successes had interesting twists.

Slim once bet that he could beat a racehorse in a hundred-yard dash. The catch was he got to choose the track. Slim cunningly chose one that was fifty yards one way and fifty yards back. By the time the racehorse was able to come to a stop, turn back around, and pick up enough speed, Slim had triumphantly crossed the finish line.

He once challenged a Taiwanese Ping-Pong champion. Slim got to choose what was used for paddles, which turned out to be Coke bottles that he had practiced with for months. Slim made quick work of the table tennis champ.

He also famously bet a bunch of suckers he could drive a golf ball over a mile. He chose a frozen lake as his course and hit a ball that glided across the ice and far into the distance, eclipsing the mile mark by a good amount.

Amarillo makes my mountain and not by the slimmest of margins.

SCOTT GAGNON

You're not supposed to know who Scott Gagnon is. He's my friend Harry's brother. Everyone in his small town of Oswego, New York (including his parents), calls him "Cow."

Cow stands about five foot nine and tips the scales at any-where from 300 to 700 pounds, depending on the supply of unlimited breadsticks in his area. His exact weight has never been recorded because he refuses to get on a scale and vice versa. If that isn't enough reason to fall deeply in love with him, in addition to his massive girth, Cow smells like fish all the time. Cow smells like fish. I know. It's getting confusing.

Even in July, when he hasn't been ice fishing for half the year, Cow still smells like carp. Also, he has forty-seven teeth in his mouth, fifteen more than the average human being. His clothes are tattered. He stands on his shoes, not in them. He constantly spits tobacco in a cup that somehow spills every few minutes. The best part of Cow is, with all he has going against him, he will make fun of others mercilessly. He is the snobbiest slob I have ever met and nothing short of a delight.

None of these things qualify him to be featured on the Mount Rushmore of gamblers, but trust me, this obese marvel can hang with the best of them in any game of chance.

Over the course of his forty-five inexplicable years on this earth, Cow has lost tens of thousands of dollars playing scratch-off lottery tickets. And that's saying a lot when you consider that he works as an onion picker on a farm (which might explain the smell as well), earning in the neighborhood of twelve bucks an hour.

The act of scratching off is the only real exercise he's ever had. That and a ridiculous dance he calls the Pig Jig that he'll sometimes do in exchange for cash, which he uses to—you guessed it—buy more scratch-off lottery tickets.

Cow's gambling versatility extends far beyond scratch-off tickets. He's also a connoisseur of Casino Night at the Elks lodge, where everyone's too disgusted to handle dice after he rolls.

And, of course, Cow plays football parlay tickets a dollar at a time. Once in a while, if he's feeling lucky, he'll risk $11 to win $10 on a college or pro-football game. And if he wins, he tells people he won $21—not because he's trying to be funny, but because he's a moron and actually thinks money recouped equals money won, which makes him, in his feeble mind, percentage-wise the greatest sports gambler of all time. He is not, of course, but still deserves a spot in pro-gambler lore.

And just for shits and giggles, here's my Mount Oddsmore as it relates to fictional characters…

TEDDY KGB IN *ROUNDERS*

Teddy KGB is not only one of the great movie gambling icons but one of the premier villains in all of cinema. John Malkovich did a marvelous job nailing this role as a Russian mobster who ran an underground Texas Hold 'Em game in New York City. Teddy KGB took no prisoners and also took Matt Damon and Edward Norton's characters for over $40,000. In the pivotal scene Damon's character sits down and plays heads-up with Teddy KGB, wiping him out for $60,000 after figuring out Teddy's tell, which came down to cookies. When KGB was bluffing or had a weak hand, he merely broke an Oreo apart. When he had a strong hand, he would devour the Oreo. The idea I guess being that he was rewarding himself with a cookie when he made the best hand or was very strong. How do you like them Oreos?

Someday I'm hoping to have enough money and time on my hands to make a prequel focusing on Teddy KGB's life and how he became so infatuated with Oreos. I'll start with the notion that his father was a Keebler Elf, fell out of a tree, and Teddy was forced to change allegiances from Keebler to Nabisco. If any studio execs are reading this right now, please contact my publisher for optioning purposes.

RAYMOND BABBITT IN *RAIN MAN*

This is the story of how a cross-dressing man named Tootsie learned to count cards to impress his brother, Lieutenant Pete "Maverick" Mitchell. Maybe I'm getting confused here. Of course this was Dustin Hoffman as Raymond Babbitt, an autistic man with savant syndrome and an incredible ability to count cards. His brother, Charlie Babbitt, played by Tom Cruise, takes him to Las Vegas to capitalize on the talent. And capitalize they did, winning $86,000 off a six-deck chute, clearing their debts before the pit bosses kicked them to the curb. Ultimately, this is not a gambling movie, but I think because I've lost so much money playing blackjack that I take great pleasure anytime the house loses.

FAST EDDIE FELSON IN *THE HUSTLER*

This one's a classic: Paul Newman as pool shark Fast Eddie Felson. I love a lot about this movie. It was shot in New York City. It costars one of my small-screen heroes, Jackie Gleason, as Minnesota Fats. And I do mean small screen. When I was twelve years old I purchased a five-inch black-and-white TV on which I only watched the Mets, *The Odd Couple*, and Jackie as Ralph Kramden in *The Honeymooners*.

Back to *The Hustler*: after running from debts, Fast Eddie hustles his way to an epic game of billiards against Minnesota Fats, beating the billiards great and earning his respect. Newman and Gleason were nominated for best actor and best supporting actor. Neither took home the Oscar, but they'll get recognized now on the Mount Oddsmore of movies, a greater achievement by any measure.

MOLLY BLOOM IN *MOLLY'S GAME*

Jessica Chastain played Molly Bloom, a former world-class skier who, through sheer determination and incredible female... balls...became the den mother of the biggest underground Hollywood poker games. Bloom, a complete badass, proved to be better than anyone else at organizing high-stakes A-list poker games. Her method of trading off debt in exchange for delinquent poker players bringing in more clients was brilliant. It all came at a cost, as the bad guys caught up to her and got physical.

I had the privilege of interviewing the real Molly Bloom on my *Against All Odds* podcast. It's probably my favorite sit-down I've ever done. I read the book and watched the Aaron Sorkin movie and came fully loaded with questions about her intriguing life. I was more excited to talk to her than I would've been any of the A-listers that played at her games.

And she didn't disappoint. Molly Bloom still has a lot to offer as an inspiration to women and business leaders everywhere. Also, Player X, whoever that may be, is a bitch.

HONORARY MENTION: HOWARD RATNER, ADAM SANDLER'S CHARACTER IN *UNCUT GEMS*

It hurts me to leave Howard Ratner out of the top four. I loved *Uncut Gems*, I love Adam Sandler, and I appreciate the fact that he took a role outside his Happy Gilmore zone.

But the last bet he made in *Uncut Gems* killed the movie for me. Sandler would've easily made the list if not for that final wager.

I was incredibly forgiving when I learned that the gem in question gave Boston Celtics star Kevin Garnett magic powers on the court.

I was okay with the time Sandler's character drove from Manhattan to Philly and made it in time before the end of the Celtics team practice.

But not even I could buy that a sportsbook would accept a wager in parlay form involving the Celtics to win the opening tip, Kevin Garnett to surpass his points and rebounds total, and the Celtics to win the game.

Anybody who knows sports gambling is aware that placing several combinations of events that are affected by each other is known as "stacking." Any casino would tell you that it's not allowed.

And, specifically, the Mohegan Sun casino, featured in

Uncut Gems, would tell you that they cannot (being based in Connecticut) take sports bets. At least, not at the time of this publication.

And if they could, they certainly wouldn't accept a six-figure bet in the form of a parlay.

If they had sent me the script, I would've flagged this nonsense immediately. And I would've done it for free. I might've even paid for the opportunity to consult.

Anyway, this is something I can't get past and that's why Howard Ratner gets a mere honorable mention.

Ah, screw it. As a half Jew I have the right to make a last-minute switch, as it relates to two members of the tribe. Sandler in! Rain Man out!

A HOT DOG HOODWINKING

The summer months are tough for sports gamblers. Staying on top of baseball is a daily marathon. And then, when you throw my Sleepy Team Theory into the mix, it becomes even more chaotic.

Here's how I see it: teams, regardless of the sport, don't show up for one-eighth of their schedule. As great as the Patriots have been through the years, there are always two weeks on their slate where after the game you're, like, *What the hell did I just see?* And it's not even necessarily after the game. You can almost spot it immediately. It was inexplicable when the lowly Jaguars would jump out to a 10–0 lead on the Pats and why Tom Brady was playing as if he'd been injected with mononucleosis. No amount of handicapping can pick this up in advance.

I'm not saying the games are rigged, although it's a fun thing to scream whenever something fishy takes place. I chalk it up to other intangible factors: collective partying the night before, not enough rest, unseen locker room mayhem. Nothing you'll read about on the injury report or see on TMZ Sports. It's just how it is.

Or maybe it's nothing at all. If you think about it, this happens not only in sports but also in all facets of life. I feel like one out of every eight times I get in my car, I'm off my game a little. I'm not mowing down dog walkers at an intersection, but I'll roll through a stop sign or forget to signal while accelerating onto a freeway on-ramp. Not because I've forgotten how to operate a motor vehicle; just one of those days.

And if you apply the Sleepy Team Theory to baseball, that 12.5 percent works out to about twenty games per year that even a great ball club isn't right. That's a tremendous amount of games to throw into the WTF category for gambling.

At any rate, I'm always looking for something other than baseball to bet on during the summer.

That's why, up until two years ago, the Nathan's Hot Dog Eating Contest served as a breath of fresh air. Joey Chestnut is the competitive-eating king. He has won the Coney Island event twelve of the last thirteen years. The one year he lost I think he got cute and challenged himself by loading up on expired relish. Actually, I don't know what happened. The point is every July Fourth, Chestnut is a prohibitive favorite. Betting on him doesn't make much sense, since you have to usually risk eight or nine bucks to win $1 back.

So the only way, within reason, to wager on the Nathan's Hot Dog Eating Contest is to play the over/under. In 2018 the projected number of wieners consumed by the winner in the men's division was set at 72.5.

Here's how I handicapped the event:

- It was expected to be a sweltering hot day in Coney Island.
- Chestnut had already set the record the previous year at seventy-two. He had nothing to prove.

So there you go. It was hot outside and Joey Chestnut was content. That was the extent of my research.

I bet a bundle on the under and then watched for ten minutes as Chestnut mowed down the field at a deliberate pace. He was eating at a steady yet slow tempo. When it was all said and done, ESPN had him at sixty-four hot dogs consumed. That meant I won by a lot. Eight and a half hot dogs...which doesn't seem like a huge amount but in reality is enough to feed the Olsen twins for three months.

And then came the post-feast interview. Chestnut was being congratulated by the master of ceremonies, an excitable man with a silly straw hat.

The interview went along unremarkably when Chestnut interrupted Mr. Funny Hat and insisted that he hadn't consumed sixty-four hot dogs as the ESPN graphics and judges indicated. He had actually eaten seventy-four. Chestnut claimed that the judges forgot to count a plate.

So what does the interviewer do? Does he defend the judges and say, "That's ridiculous, Joey—you're delirious from the massive nitrate intake"? Does he say, "Well, we'll go to the videotape and get back to you a few bowel movements from now"?

No. Neither of those things. He celebrates the statement

and announces that with seventy-four consumed hot dogs Joey Chestnut has broken his own world record. The crowd goes nuts and my money goes up in Fourth of July fireworks.

To give you a little context, this is like if after game six of the NBA Finals we bore witness to this interview:

Doris Burke: Steph Curry, your team bowed out to the Raptors in six games. You came up just short... 114–110. This must be very disappointing to you.

Steph Curry: Actually, Doris, I know the ABC graphic had us scoring 110 points, but we really scored 120.

Doris Burke: One hundred and twenty points for the Golden State Warriors!!! They win game 6. We'll see you for game 7 Sunday in Toronto!!!

It's hard to imagine that the Nathan's Hot Dog Eating Contest, the most American event imaginable, would end in such gambling chaos. It would be easy enough for me to blame Russian meddling or that the judges fell victim to the Sleepy Team Theory, but I think the moral of the story is to, God forbid, take the summer off from gambling and enjoy your family.

MOST RIDICULOUS EVENTS TO WAGER ON

CUSTOMER RECEIPT

Pro-wrestling matches (even)

Awards shows (3/1)

Competitive-eating competitions (8/1)

Your son's little league games (25/1)

Win total:

Total bet:

65988 - 4 480780244354 5 379045345- 3 678 4534 3 -4 678 678353 678534

HEDGING YOUR BETS: AN IRRATIONAL USER'S GUIDE

People, mostly men, stop me at urinals all the time to ask, "How do you hedge a big bet?"

First of all, now that I've completed about 80 percent of this memoir, I should probably let you know that it's pointless to ever ask me advice on gambling. Often I don't parlay what I preach.

Case in point: Super Bowl XXXVI between the Rams and Patriots. My cousin Jimmy was giving pregame picks on *Fox NFL Sunday*. I would often advise him on his selections but this one seemed simple. The Rams were a 13-point favorite and at that time Jimmy was only allowed to pick winners on the show.

Since the spread didn't factor in, it made sense to pick the

Rams who, by Vegas's calculations, had over a 90 percent chance of emerging victorious. I got in his ear before taping the segment and advised him to take the Patriots to win. My reasoning was that if New England pulled off the upset, he would look like a genius. If they lost—well, it was a long off-season and people would forgive and forget by the following September when he was back giving picks.

Jimmy took my advice and chose the 7/1 underdog Patriots. We were actually at the game in New Orleans when Adam Vinatieri kicked the ball perfectly through the goalposts, giving the Pats their first Lombardi Trophy.

Jimmy pumped his fist, celebrating, only to look down to see me with my head in my hands.

Jimmy: Get up and celebrate. Our pick won!

Me: That was *your* pick. I had $5,000 on the Rams to win the game.

So there you go. You should take everything I say with a grain of cyanide. But as far as hedging goes, I can at least take you through the basics. For those of you who are new to the gaming game, "hedging" is defined as (I'm taking the first thing that pops up on Google) "placing a bet or bets on a different outcome to your original bet to secure a guaranteed profit regardless of the result, or reduce your risk on a market."

Here's what hedging amounts to in a nutshell. Let's say before the season starts you put in a $100 bet on the Chiefs to win the Super Bowl at 7/1 odds. Kansas City survives the regular season, the playoffs, and then the big game rolls around. You stand to win $700 if the Chiefs emerge victorious. How much do you bet (if anything) on the 49ers to hedge against your winnings?

As far as I'm concerned, the answer depends on a lot of factors.

1. IS THE WAGER WORTHY OF PLACING A HEDGE BET?

Anything 2/1 odds or less is probably not worth it. That is, if you stand to win less than double your money hedging a bet, you might just want to let it go. Remember this rule of thumb: the more bets you place, the better off for the house. And not the house you pay a mortgage on every month. The ones in Vegas with all the pretty lights.

But in the example I gave above, at 7/1 odds, you should definitely at least consider hedging your $700 potential outcome if you're affected by all or some of the following factors.

2. IS YOUR FINANCIAL SITUATION ONE THAT WOULD DEEM IT BENEFICIAL FOR YOU TO HEDGE?

Keep in mind that we're all supposed to be betting responsibly. But if Jeff Bezos walks into a sportsbook (stop me if you've heard this one already) and makes that Chiefs bet and is poised to win $700, he's probably not going to hedge. Losing his initial investment isn't going to make the slightest of dents in his

Amazon empire. He'd probably up-charge you on the cost of this book to cover it. So he's fine.

Conversely, if the guy who played Screech on *Saved by the Bell* finds a ticket with that Chiefs at 7/1 futures bet on it, it might be wise for him to gather up as many empty Shasta cola cans as he can, redeem them, and use the loot to bet a few hundred bucks on the 49ers so as to guarantee an equal payout regardless of the outcome.

3. HOW IS YOUR LUCK IN GENERAL?

If you're the kind of person who drives around the mall for hours looking for a parking space to no avail or who, over the course of their life, has misplaced over 37.5 pairs of sunglasses and has never won a thing, and you're staring at a 7/1 payout or nothing if it loses…it's probably a good idea to hedge. Odds are decent that you're not going to hit pay dirt, and if you do, it's only going to mean the sunglasses you lose will be the expensive Ray-Bans.

I don't even want to go into how many times Bill Simmons and I had the opportunity to hedge. We RARELY ever hedged and RARELY ever won our original bets.

4. ARE YOU SUPERSTITIOUS?

Last year I interviewed a fellow named Scott Berry on my *Against All Odds* podcast. Scott's story is a great one. He and his buddies went to Vegas on a work trip in January 2019. Rather than blow it at the blackjack table, Scott did the responsible thing. He headed to the Paris sportsbook and put all $400 of his allotted weekend gambling money on his beloved St. Louis Blues at 250/1 odds to win the Stanley Cup. The Blues, at the time, were in last place, with the worst record in hockey. Make no mistake about it, this was a stupid bet of epic proportions. It's the kind of wager you make when you're blackout drunk and stumbling back to your hotel from a Molly-induced after-hours rager in Henderson.

Except that it wasn't stupid at all. The Blues proceeded to go on a legendary 30-10-5 run to end the regular season. And just like that, Scott's ticket had a prayer of cashing.

In the first round of the playoffs the Blues finished off the Winnipeg Jets in six games. Then came the conference semifinals. They knocked out the Dallas Stars in seven. Now Scott starts getting serious offers for his futures ticket: $5,000, $10,000. Someone even offered PropSwap (a futures ticket broker) $20,000 for his bet. Scott would pocket twenty grand (minus the $400 investment) and just watch as a fan the rest of the way while someone else sweated out the $100K outcome. But Scott ignored the offers and the Blues kept rolling.

The Blues had a lot going for them, in addition to Scott's undying faith. They had an outstanding rookie goaltender in Jordan Binnington, who sounded more like a British theater actor than a flawless netminder. They had a rally song: Laura Branigan's "Gloria," which would play after every home victory. Not exactly "We Are the Champions," but it was part of the fun, which was really amped up after the Blues beat the Sharks in six to make the Stanley Cup finals.

Degenerates were coming out of the woodwork to take this legendary ticket off Scott's hands. An offer of $41,000 came before game 1. Another for $48,000 before game 3 (when the series was tied 1–1).

Let's stop and think about this for a second. That $48,000 represents almost half what Scott stood to win and 192 times his initial investment. This is the equivalent of Forrest Gump never unloading his Apple stock. Scott could've landed season tickets on the ice and still had enough money left over to purchase the Zamboni. Ninety-nine percent of those hanging on to this ticket would've said good-bye to it. Not Scott. He held firm.

I was intrigued by this gutsy and puzzling man. I hate hedging but even I felt it was my obligation to talk some sense into him. The series was tied 3–3. With one game, winner take all, remaining in the season Scott was now being offered $50K for his futures bet. Over one hundred times his investment. I interviewed him the night before game 7.

But my heart-to-heart with Scott was fruitless. I wasn't talking him into or out of anything. He had already heard the same, very reasonable advice from everyone close to him. When I pressed him on his decision not to budge, Scott chalked his stubbornness up to superstition. The Blues were Scott's team and he rightly pointed out that good things started happening to his team immediately after he placed the bet.

The hedge offers were a nonfactor. In Scott's mind, everything would go sideways if he altered the original Vegas wager even in the slightest.

This was a ridiculously impractical way of thinking, yet I loved everything about it. I finished the interview with this query, taking any and all economic logic out of the equation:

"If tonight someone were to offer you the full $100,000 for the $400 ticket, would you take it?"

Scott hesitated and then said he'd have to think about it.

The fact that he hesitated is all you need to know about fandom. Scott Berry became an instant hero of mine—even before the St. Louis Blues celebrated after winning the Stanley Cup, netting him $99,600 on a futures bet.

Scott instilled in me two lessons I thought I had already learned.

The first is that deep down all we ever secretly want is to believe we have control over our team's fate. None of us does, but this is as close as it gets to being able to convince yourself otherwise.

The second lesson is that the age-old adage is true: hedging is for gardeners.

ESCAPE FROM THE BLACK HOLE

This year the Oakland Raiders picked up and moved their team to Las Vegas. It made sense on a lot of levels, and yet this is very surprising, considering the NFL's previous unshakable stance on anything Vegas or gambling related.

Commissioner Roger Goodell took such a hard line you would think one of Siegfried and Roy's white tigers had mauled his favorite aunt. (RIP Roy.) He was an even bigger stickler when it came to gambling on football. Goodell famously said that the NFL "remains very much opposed to legalized gambling on sports." This wasn't twenty years ago; this was in the mid-2010s. Now the Raiders are in Vegas.

An estimated $6 billion was bet last year on the Super Bowl alone, and I guarantee that doesn't even count bets with Harry on who the MVP is going to thank first, his teammates or God.

There is no denying fantasy football. Daily fantasy sites such as FanDuel and Draftkings are a huge reason the NFL thrives.

Lesley Visser's coming-of-age interview with Drew Brees is swell, but the overwhelming majority of NFL fans wake up and want to know two things: Who am I putting in my fantasy lineup and which team am I betting?

So it makes sense that the Raiders would move to Vegas from Oakland, a place where I incurred one of the most horrifying professional experiences in my life.

Let me set the stage. Last fall I had, like, seventeen jobs. I was basically a fat Ryan Seacrest. I was cohosting *Lock It In*, a live daily sports gambling show on Fox Sports 1. I had two podcasts, one on which I guessed the NFL spreads for the upcoming week with Bill Simmons and another more focused on sports gambling with my childhood buddies Darren, Harry, and Brian, who I affectionately refer to as the Degenerate Trifecta. I was appearing in hidden camera and man-on-the-street bits for *Jimmy Kimmel Live!* and was responsible for writing and starring in a comedy bit that aired on the pregame show Thursday nights on Fox. Oh, and I was supposed to be writing this book, which by now, after reading several chapters, you can surmise I tackled in sort of a half-assed manner.

I am actually typing these words from my son Archie's first high school wrestling tournament. If the words "Get wrist control, goddamn it" pop up—you'll know why.

That's how tight time is. Trust me, I'm not complaining. This is the greatest life anyone in my position could ask for. It just becomes a little hectic when you're doing radio interviews from the toilet.

Back in November 2019, juggling these tasks and making a trip to Oakland was already going to be challenging. Fox wanted me to travel every other week to the Thursday night venue and I did my best to accommodate. The comedy bit idea in Oakland was to go to a bar and read fake tweets from real celebrities to rabid Raiders fans in an effort to elicit angry reactions.

I posted on my Twitter account asking Raiders fans to come to a downtown bar for a chance to be on the Fox pregame show. The result was nothing short of miraculous. I have over 200,000 Twitter followers and exactly zero of them showed up. There were three guys in the whole place watching Man U and Tottenham. Had I approached them about real football, they likely would've spit a mouthful of fish and chips in my face.

It was unfathomable. Not one diehard was interested in being on TV? Have we gotten to a point where every American has appeared on television? Maybe we have. I felt like deleting my Twitter account on the spot. What would I miss, really? A few Michael Jordan sad face memes and the president harassing Bette Midler? That was strike one for me and Oakland.

Anyway, I held on to the account, and we regrouped and traveled to a real Raiders bar about ten miles away called Ricky's. The owner, a sixty-five-year-old woman not named Ricky, was a fan of mine. When we arrived, she immediately got on her Facebook page and called for all her lunatic friends with Raiders gear to come down. We hired her as an associate producer.

In a matter of minutes, dozens of maniacal fans showed up and they each had a few choice words for Bill Belichick, the mayor of Oakland, and several other public figures, including Pope Francis, who some actually believed tweeted the words " 'I would say to pray for Raiders fans, but really, what's the point?' #YouGotPoped."

We had our bit. Now I just had to stick around for a *Lock*

It In taping and then my live hit from the stadium. My end of *Lock It In* would be taped in a small conference room in the Intercontinental Hotel in San Francisco. I would go on live from 1:30 to 2:30 and then get shuttled over the bridge to Oakland–Alameda County Coliseum, which sounds a lot more majestic than it is. More on that in a bit.

I got dressed, reviewed my notes, and made it to the conference room for *Lock It In* only to learn of a few stumbling blocks.

First off, my hair/makeup dude went to the stadium instead of the hotel. An honest mistake. It happens all the time, and by that I mean it really never happens ever. As a result our poor little cable TV audience would be subjected to my pasty pudgy face. To add insult to injury, my *Lock It In* backplate—that's a TV background for this impromptu set—was delayed in the California wildfires and never made it to the conference room. The on-site technician had to rig up a black background that resembled a wall. So with a shiny face and dull background I was all of a sudden presenting the most overproduced public-access show of all time.

Oh, and the three-second satellite delay wasn't great when my cohosts Rachel Bonnetta, Clay Travis, and Todd Fuhrman made fun of all of the above. Strike two.

But whatever: I got through it, changed shirts, and jumped in the car with Norm, my Fox producer, and Brother Bri, my *Against All Odds* cohost, who was a lifelong Raiders fan. I told Bri to come out, seeing as this would likely be the final time he could walk on the field. He was delighted to be there.

So Bri and I jump into Norm's car at around 2:45 p.m. for what should've been a twenty-five-minute ride over the bridge into Oakland.

You may ask why I didn't play it safe and stay in Oakland if that's where my big moment was going down.

The answer is: by anyone's metrics, staying in Oakland is hardly playing it safe.

I did what anyone with over $17 to their name would do and secured a hotel room in San Francisco. Besides, I had a 4:48 live hit and the ride to the stadium should've taken forty minutes at most. Departing at 2:45 would give me plenty of time, except for the part where I wouldn't be writing about this if that were the case.

As soon as we attempted the ramp for the bridge, we could see that it was backed up for miles. Traffic was at a complete standstill. But I remained calm, as we still had an hour and forty minutes before the cameras were hot. But then forty-five minutes later when we hadn't moved a furlong, I started to panic. I urged my producer, who was from Canada, to start driving like an asshole American. Norm all of a sudden injected himself with some Brooklyn courage and cut a few rubberneckers off, and eventually we made it onto the bridge by about 4:00 p.m.

We reached the other side around 4:15, leaving me thirty-three minutes to travel three miles. Game night traffic slammed us again. With eighteen minutes remaining we were still a mile away.

Brother Bri and I decided to ditch the car and run the rest of the way to the stadium. The only problem was that between us and the field were dozens of con artists trying to sell, buy, or maybe steal tickets.

"Who's got? Who needs?"

It got worse when a few of them spotted my Fox badge.

"Oh, look at pretty boy over here trying to race to the

game with his Fox badge. Maybe I'll just take that from you, pretty boy."

I've never been described as pretty but wasn't willing to stop and see if the gentleman with the tattooed eyeballs was referring to me. I remained focused and kept running. It was all starting to seem like a bad dream and a video game put together. A lot like Super Mario Brothers but in this case the Sidesteppers were addicted to meth.

"Tell Howie Long to kiss my ass."

It was a message I didn't plan to pass on even in the unlikely event I made it to the field alive.

Foot traffic lightened up and we made it to the building at 4:30. I got lucky when a couple of security guards mercifully gave us the right directions, and by 4:39 I was on the field. The wrong side of the field.

I sprinted the final one hundred yards like Bo Jackson post–hip injury and made it to my spot with four minutes to spare. That gave me time to get mic'd up, catch my breath, and shoot the shit with Gorilla Rilla, one of the original members of the Raider crazies who we had seen the day before at Ricky's.

I was a sweaty disaster of a mess, but as I looked up and saw the dudes with the spiked shoulder pads and painted faces, I was convinced that even with drenched armpits and messed-up hair I wasn't going to stand out.

I could make out Buck and Aikman in my earpiece, which was a good sign. Howie Long and Michael Strahan were able to hear me during my mic check, so I was in good shape.

Two minutes to showtime and I still had to complete my bravest feat to date, climbing into the first row of the south end zone, otherwise known as the Black Hole. There I would be surrounded by arrogant screaming fanatics with body odor and painted-up facial hair. And that was just the women. The men were even more terrifying. One minute to go, when I felt a hand, not mine, make its way into my back pocket. I keep my wallet in my front pocket, so the derelict behind me wasn't getting my money. But my back pocket contained a written tally of all the bets I had made throughout the week/month, which may have been more valuable than anything in my wallet. I reached back and grabbed the hand of the lowlife trying to pickpocket me and turned his wrist upward using whatever dumb judo move I remembered from college. I whipped around and this menacing nut job is smiling at me. I say to him firmly...

"Hey, jackass, we're on live TV in forty-five seconds. Do you think you can fucking behave yourself?"

The ogre just kept laughing. I turned back around as I was counted into the segment.

Three...two...one...live

I read one more fake tweet, this one from Howie Long:

"Howie Long tweets... what does a Raiders fan do after winning the Super Bowl? He turns off his Xbox and goes to bed."

This infuriated the Black Hole. I gave my pick for the game, Raiders over Chargers (turned out to be a winner), and got the fuck out of there.

Brother Bri and I had access to seats in the press box, but we also got a few minutes to hang out on the field. Bri got to see his favorite Raiders stretch and clown each other. Not long after the live hit, we were approached by the president of the Raiders, Marc Badain. Mark was a big fan of my podcast with Simmons. We made small talk and I told him about the incident in the Black Hole. He told me I was lucky to have my limbs, let alone my wallet. After a few minutes of friendly chatter, Mark handed me and Bri tickets to his luxury suite. It was a very nice gesture.

We followed him up and went inside. Let's put it this way: it wasn't as nice as any other luxury box I had seen on television—we were still in Oakland Coliseum, mind you—but was a step up from the tiny conference room where I had shot *Lock It In* earlier in the day.

We watched the game from there and eventually I had to use the restroom. You're not going to believe this, but there was no restroom in the luxury box—I guess peeing is too luxurious, so I walked out and used the bathroom where the commoners relieved themselves. Another war zone. Smoke of all kinds filled the air. A Chargers fan was getting shoved and harassed at the urinal. I decided to take a pass on the piss and wandered over to the concession stand to buy a pretzel.

I couldn't hope to notice their choice of beverages: RC Cola, Sunkist, and Hawaiian Punch lemonade.

Strike three for Oakland.

It may be time for everyone in Oakland to move to Vegas.

WORST PLACES TO WATCH A SPORTING EVENT

CUSTOMER RECEIPT

Oakland (–350)

Rwanda (4/1)

Kabul (6/1)

Under a table at a family wedding with your angry mother-in-law (12/1)

Win total: _____

Total bet: _____

65988 - 4 4807802443545 379045345- 3 678 4534 3 -4 678 678353 678534

THE WISDOM OF THE GRIDIRON

You would hardly know it from looking at me now, but back in the day, high school athletics kept me pretty fit. It was football in the fall and wrestling in the winter. I'll credit wrestling with giving me a drill instructor state of mind that comes in handy every eighteen months or so, when I summon the discipline to lose twenty pounds only to gain it all right back in three trips to an all-you-can-eat Brazilian barbecue.

But aside from that, there wasn't much to love about wrestling. Sucking pounds as a fifteen-year-old to avoid stud wrestlers in higher weight classes was just plain dumb. Staring at the gym ceiling while a referee slammed his hand on a mat lathered in impetigo wasn't too bright, either.

I wasn't very good and had to get creative to make up for my lack of skills. Sometimes I would load up on beans and broccoli, thinking I could build up enough gas to blast my opponent into submission.

Once I doused my singlet in Drakkar Noir, hoping for a similar result. But it never really worked. In fact, I think it inspired my opponents to make quicker work of me than they normally did.

Wrestling wasn't fun for me.

But football was different. I loved everything about it. I loved the smell of the grass on Saturdays. I even loved the musk of a locker room where almost nobody washed their practice equipment for a full three months.

The football coaches were the best. I don't want to call him out by name, but our head coach whose name rhymed with Schmeverett Schmelius was an absolute basket case.

It was amazing how little I learned from this obese nut job. First off, Schmelius hated water, or at least hated allowing his players to drink. During two-a-day practices in the summer, Schmelius begrudgingly let us sip from the hose once every two-and-a-half hours and would watch over you like a hawk to make sure you didn't drink for more than two or three seconds. It was barely enough time to get your lips wet. His argument was that water gave you cramps and he didn't want a bunch of kids cramping up during practice—which is weird, because I once read somewhere that water also hydrates you. But, honestly, how important could something like hydration be in 95-degree heat? Whatever his reasoning, let's just say Coach Schmelius wasn't getting a Poland Spring endorsement deal anytime soon.

His lack of smarts wasn't limited to hydration. Coach Schmelius ran a very dull, predictable, and unsuccessful offense for the John Glenn Knights. He called for running plays about 137 percent of the time. It didn't matter if it was first and ten or third and fifteen. Bull 2 wedge up the middle was the go-to play. His reasoning was "If you put the ball in the air, three things can happen, and two of them are bad."

The bad being incomplete and interception. But the same goes for handing off, where you can suffer no gain or a fumble.

It's ridiculous logic anyway. It's like saying you shouldn't cross the street because two of the three results are bad. Sure, you could get from one side to another, but you could also trip and fall into a manhole or get hit by a bus. Coach's philosophy was "Always stay exactly where you are."

We were stuck with this vanilla offense for years. It was a shame, too, because one of my best friends, Darren, was a solid quarterback with a cannon who lit up the practice field. But it didn't matter to our fearless coach and his caveman game plan.

As far as motivational speakers went, there were none more confusing than Schmelius. His favorite rallying cry was "the six Ps." "Prior planning prevents piss-poor performances," he used to say, and then look around as if he was expecting high fives from the group.

One day I put a pin in his brilliance when I raised my hand and pointed out that he could simplify it to "the five Ps," since "prior planning" was redundant. Everyone got a kick out of the correction except for Schmelius.

I just couldn't leave well enough alone. At football camp the sophomores had to perform skits. I staged a Piper's Pit, an interview show in which I pretended to be my boyhood idol, Rowdy Roddy Piper. It was during this interview that I called Schmelius out for getting angry with the catering staff for not supplying brownies to sate his sweet tooth. We couldn't have water, but he demanded baked goods. Made sense. We all snickered to ourselves about it until I pointed it out to his face. I presented him, in Rowdy Roddy fashion, with a plate of brownies, and the rest of the team and coaches lost it.

But Schmelius had a plan for me. He was going to get me back good. The starting kickoff team would have to practice their drills. On any other high school team they would run these drills against the second team kick return squad. Well, we kind of did that, too, except Schmelius had me returning with one blocker instead of ten.

Poor Gino Gradziedei was the sacrificial lamb who would get pummeled immediately before I got trampled.

Gino didn't deserve it. He was fine with the six Ps. He never even touched the brownies.

But I guess zero blockers would have been too cruel, so Gino was the first line of defense before everyone took a shot at my 140-pound frame.

The kickoff drill was the first one we would run every day after stretches. I remember getting nervous about this starting at seventh period. It was like going to a slaughterhouse every day.

But the joke was on Schmelius, as when we kicked off in our first real game against Amityville, former Syracuse great (and Jets so-so) Rob Carpenter took it to the house for ninety yards and a touchdown. That's the kind of thing that happens when a team isn't used to getting blocked. They fell like statues. Schmelius loses again.

But it wasn't all bad on the John Glenn coaching staff. Ron Scudder was an assistant coach I enjoyed very much. He understood me and on some level appreciated me and my friend Sneaky Joe. Joey and I had "Scuds" for physics, and were so disruptive he made us sit on opposite ends of the classroom. He called us the Goof Brothers and claimed we shouldn't be in the same ion, let alone the same classroom. Scuds was a piece of work, too. He claimed he was the third alternate to Christa McAuliffe's spot. McAuliffe was the teacher-astronaut who unfortunately met her demise in the space shuttle *Challenger*. He would remind us all the time that we were lucky it wasn't him.

Scuds was into shenanigans himself. He once gave me, and only me, a physics test that was written in Korean. I swear to God, I was so woefully unprepared for the quiz that I had to look at it for a good ten-Mississippi count before I figured out I was being pranked. I was almost convinced that the symbols were equations I hadn't studied.

One Saturday, half the varsity football team—the ones who thought they could get into college—were taking the SAT at around the same time we had a game scheduled with Hampton Bays. Scuds was in charge of getting all of the SAT takers on a bus for the one-hour ride to Quogue on the east end of Long Island in the hopes that we could make it for the last three quarters of the game. We probably should've just forfeited, but Scuds had an ironclad plan to make it work. Part of that plan was to alert the bus driver to various shortcuts so that we could make up some time. Well, one of these shortcuts went awry and led us down Old Depot Road, which ended up having no outlet. We drove for twenty minutes, and when we hit the dead end, we laughed and celebrated as if we had won the Long Island Class A championship.

We eventually wished we had kept quiet, because Scuds spent the next three weeks bringing in maps from 1937 showing that Old Depot Road actually had an outlet. Scuds was hell-bent on being right.

I loved dumb stories like these.

As far as the game itself, football is the most intense team sport. It teaches camaraderie like none other. You really can't put a value on the lessons you learn persevering through exhaustion and injury with your peers—and that's really what it was all about. Not to mention the possibility that, if you were wearing your varsity jacket, a pretty girl would pass you in the halls and stare at you for a second or two without making a disgusted look.

That was a nice experience, and so naturally I wanted my oldest son, Archie, to share the joy that came along with playing organized tackle football.

He was already in love with the game. One of his favorite things to do was to lay out when I tossed him the pigskin on the beach. By age twelve he was already in three fantasy football leagues. He played flag football in the fall and spring but got bored with it, mainly because the better kids went off to play tackle football.

He was ready. My wife, Melissa, wasn't. She was understandably worried. Tackle football isn't as acceptable as it was when I played in the late eighties. Perception of the dangers of the game have changed. Every week there was a new article or documentary or HBO *Real Sports* episode featuring concussion talk, and it was never good.

Bryant Gumbel should donate three-quarters of his salary to chronic traumatic encephalopathy (CTE) research, since that seems to be all his show focuses on.

But the numbers don't lie. A recent study determined that out of 266 deceased former players who had their brains tested,

223 were found to meet the criteria for CTE—about 83 percent. The risk of CTE is said to double every 2.6 years of playing tackle football.

So where does that leave me as a father? Am I that much of a frustrated athlete that I can't look at the obvious and make a logical decision? I definitely had a couple concussions myself: it's going to happen when you're fighting off eleven idiot teammates who are trying to crush you. I didn't think of it as anything other than a bad headache—similar to when you attend a Marilyn Manson concert or a Slurpee-eating convention—but the truth is it's much worse and I was very fortunate to not have a lasting condition.

I had to be responsible but thought I could come up with a fair solution regarding Archie's participation.

I came up with this: one concussion and he'd be out.

If he lasted four years without one, God bless. If he got dinged once, he'd have to quit.

It seemed wise. And to prove to my wife that it was a fair trade-off, I got help from a pro.

While this debate was raging, my cousin Jimmy had set up a dinner with Cowboys great/broadcaster Tony Romo and our wives. Romo had taken his share of hits and not only had his wits about him but also was now considered to be the best color commentator in the game. His brain was firing on all neurons. I had to seize this opportunity.

We got to the restaurant and hadn't even decided on sparkling or flat water before I popped the question.

Me: Tony, my oldest wants to play tackle football. I want to let him play until he gets one concussion. That's fine, right?

Romo: How old is he?

Me: He's twelve.

Romo (hesitates): Ehhh…he can start playing around junior year in high school.

What?!?!?!?!?! Junior year was four seasons from that meal.

I can forgive Romo for the botched handling of a snap in that playoff game against Seattle and the stupid Skechers commercials, but this was a betrayal that was going to take time to get over.

The whole table laughed at my overreaction, which made me think Romo was pulling a practical joke on me.

But he wasn't. Romo went on to explain that the hits were a real thing and if you were already skittish and your child didn't need to learn technique as an offensive lineman, he could probably wait until sixteen or so to play. It made sense but was not the answer I was expecting or needed to hear.

Melissa and I decided to split the difference between Romo's suggestion and my proposal. Archie would wait two years before putting the pads on, even though most of his friends were already playing. By age fifteen and a solid six foot one (even though there's no height whatsoever in my family and I try to ignore the fact that he bears a striking resemblance to my wife's favorite Door Dash driver), he's playing football and loves it every bit as much as I thought he would.

Archie has never once complained about double practices in the summer. He fills in at whatever position the coach needs him, regardless of his personal preference. He studies his playbook like a prisoner studies a *Penthouse* magazine.

And he's good. One of the best tacklers on his team. He

wears number 56 in honor of Lawrence Taylor. There are a few things I need to tell him about LT, but those can wait a couple of years.

Everything was going great until recently when one of his teammates caught a screen pass, turned upfield, and was immediately met with a helmet-to-helmet hit by a kid who was a foot taller. The poor little guy's legs were flailing while his upper body showed no movement. Both teams took a knee and prayed together for forty minutes until the paramedics arrived and stretchered him over to the local hospital.

It was a terrifying time that thankfully turned out fine. The kid ended up with a minor neck injury and was back in school two days later.

The whole thing reminded me of sex in that, afterward, my wife couldn't bear to look me in the eye for over an hour. Never once was she concerned about me and how this kind of thing affects my brand. So selfish.

Kidding aside, this incident really hit home. I would've lost my mind if it was Archie out there. We had a conversation. He wanted to continue and I told him to forget about the one concussion rule. If at any point he didn't feel it was worth it, he could walk away with no judgment passed.

This was also right around the time Indianapolis Colts quarterback Andrew Luck retired. Luck was praised for taking $15 million and going home. Who am I to say my own son, who wasn't being compensated beyond free Wi-Fi at home, shouldn't be able to make this decision for himself?

When it comes to safety precautions regarding organized football, there are lots of maybe's out there. Maybe we should all be deathly afraid of the potential damage. Maybe Romo has it right in suggesting that you should wait as long as you can to play in order to cut down on the risk. Maybe playing exactly one year of high school football is enough to whet your appetite without pushing the limits for the greatest team sport around. And maybe Coach Schmelius should've been slapped with attempted murder charges for forcing me to return kicks with one blocker. Actually, that one I'm almost certain of.

ALWAYS END ON
A LOW NOTE

I don't want to spend too much time on the coronavirus stuff because (a) it's depressing as shit, and (b) this chapter will seem dated no matter how long I put off writing it. I hope.

I'll say a few things, though. On Thursday, March 12, around 10:00 a.m.—as was routine for every weekday—I was preparing for *Lock It In*, my sports gambling talk show. Things were already very sketchy in the sports world, as the night before Utah Jazz center Rudy Gobert vomited before a game and subsequently tested positive for Covid-19. The game was canceled immediately. Hours passed and video emerged of Gobert "clowning" his teammates by touching all of the microphones in a press conference. It was not unlike what my cohost Rachel Bonnetta and I had done a few days earlier when we snuck into our boss Charlie's office and took pictures pretending to lick his sports Emmys and then sent him the photos.

During the show the week before, our cohost Todd Fuhrman coughed and we all had a big laugh.

Clay: Uh-oh, Fuhrman just coughed. Were you in China, Fuhrman?

Rachel: Oh, no…quarantine time.

Sal: Whoa—even odds that he has the big C.

We were all so naïve and insensitive. Most Americans were. Our leaders failed to educate us about the reach of the virus.

On that Thursday the twelfth, the call came in that our show and all programs on the lot that day were canceled as of Friday and the foreseeable future.

This was insane.

I stopped preparing and tuned in to the St. John's–Creighton game, where the first half was winding down. While most others were searching online for disinfectant, I scurried to locate a bet. I found it. St. John's +6 in the second half. I had to do it. I placed a substantial amount on the second-half wager, knowing that it could be my last one for a long while. Within minutes of my wager, the Big East commissioner canceled the rest of the game. The other NCAA conferences followed and soon all of sports was dead.

For the next two months we were presented with an avalanche of terrible sports gambling substitutes. A couple days into the pandemic, I found a site that hosted virtual camel racing and promptly lost $90. After that, I was betting on NBA players in H-O-R-S-E competitions. Other simulations were offered as alternative gambling options. It was all so depressing. I placed ninth out of twenty in a WNBA draft pool and was excited about it. It was beyond pathetic.

I tried to keep things fresh with my audience by offering a $100 gift card to whoever came closest to guessing the combined total of the numbers in the Powerball drawing. This ended up being a disaster, as people came out of the woodwork complaining they had guessed the number even though it didn't show up in my Twitter timeline. With my future employment being uncertain I had to make sure I didn't go broke and discontinued the contest.

My workdays were reduced to hosting podcasts featuring "best of" moments from big sporting events from the past. Once in a while my *Lock It In* team and I would provide digital posts previewing the upcoming season. When the NFL forged ahead with their schedule release, we were asked to preview the odds for the week 1 NFL games in September. We had to do our best to pretend to have an edge on games that might or might not be played 120 days in advance.

I often get a kick out of my kids screaming at the top of their lungs, pretending to call fake matches they were creating with their wrestling action figures. Now they were laughing at me.

But the last thing I want is to look like I'm complaining. This is why I hesitated to write this chapter. With the exception of the few times I looked for heavy-ish objects to throw at my misbehaving children, this quarantine has been fine for me. I promise, I'm appreciative for the things that I have, especially when tens of millions have lost their jobs and hundreds of thousands of Americans have perished. Bellyaching about not having sports to gamble on is lame, so I try to keep it in check.

It's still early and there's talk of second and third waves and horrible shit to come. But I remain positive about the future and take solace in the fact that we have the smartest people in the world working 24/7 to find a vaccine. And that at the very least, if things get hairy again, you have my permission to use the contents of this book as a toilet paper substitute.

My cousin Jimmy just read the book and gave me this note in big red letters: "THIS CANNOT BE HOW YOU END THE BOOK." He's right, and I realize it's a bummer of a chapter and I should probably summarize with something profound. But I've been at it for forty-five minutes now and just can't think of the right words to wrap this up, so let me just end by posting a blurry screen grab of me vomiting up oysters during my competitive eating contest versus Joe House.

And that's that.

ACKNOWLEDGMENTS

There are far too many people for me to acknowledge. Dozens upon dozens of friends and family members kept me focused and provided me with the insight and remarkable antics that helped me plot out this memoir. It's much easier to list the names of people who *didn't* have any influence over me and the writing of this book. So here it goes:

Shia LaBeouf

Katherine Heigl

That's a cop-out. Here's the real list of influencers I'd like to express my appreciation for:

My wife, Melissa—my Rooster. She's given me kindness, patience, stability, and the three best kids in the world. And she was able to pull all of this off while navigating the last two decades through a cloud of farts.

My sons, Archie, Jack, and Harrison, for never thinking to jump on the massive Word document that turned out to be my book or inserting juvenile penis references while I wasn't looking. I know—at their ages I would not have had the same restraint.

My mother, Fran Iacono, who actually got me interested in writing by penning a "Have a great day, sweetheart" message on the napkin that accompanied my Hebrew National salami sandwich every day of kindergarten.

My father, Vincent Iacono, who by going on a business trip to Texas and subsequently bringing home a Dallas Cowboys jacket for his seven-year-old son all but guaranteed that boy would never be forced to root for the lowly New York Jets.

My sisters, Ivy and Teddi, for toughing it out and never requesting medical attention during their early years as I practiced my pro wrestling moves on them in the basement.

My grandparents, Sal and Edith Iacono and George and Millie Gunther, for settling in New York—the illegal gambling capital of the world.

My cousin Jimmy Kimmel for giving me every big break to access this insane life and for the unfortunate yet accurate words provided in his foreword.

All of my cousins and cousins-in-law, who will always be like brothers and sisters and Saloobs to me.

My aunts Chippy and Joan and uncles Frank and Jimmy for *their* various addictions to nurturing, smoking, gambling, cooking, worrying, and driving people to the airport.

Harry Gagnon, Darren Szokoli, and Brian Szokoli for being the best sports gambling partners this degenerate could ask for.

The Sports-ish Guy Bill Simmons for leading the charge in our ongoing anti-hedge campaign.

James "Baby Doll" Dixon for taking only 10 percent of my scribe earnings despite all the calls (one) that he made in arranging my book deal.

Joey Conza, Chris Nahas, Jon Finkin, and Frank Tassone just for being the boyzzz.

Daniel Kellison, who came up with the catchy title of this book and who—along with Tony Barbieri and Donick Cary—is responsible for setting me up with my extraordinary wife.

Rowdy Roddy Piper for giving me a good ass kicking when I needed it and for leaving me with a lifetime supply of bubble gum.

Brad Mulcahy for serving as an inspiration to fight through adversity and for keeping me entertained beyond football on Sundays.

Don Barris and Perry Caravello, my favorite comedy couple.

The New York State Bar Association for failing me both times I took the bar exam. This book would've been a lot more boring had they let me through.

The rest in no particular order (fine...celebrities first):

Adam Carolla	David Chang
Huey Lewis	Yehya
The News	The Vault
Jeffrey Ross	Ken Kestenbaum
Super Dave Osborne	Rachel Bonnetta
Ben Stein	Todd Fuhrman
Dicky Barrett	Clay Travis
Neil Everett	Charlie Dixon
Stan Verrett	Gino Graziadei
Tony Romo	Dr. Bruce
Melrose Larry Green	Mario Bosco
Lenny Dykstra	Joe House

John Carlin

Erin Irwin

Hotter

Weeno

Lloyd

Louis D'Ambrosio

Scott Gagnon

Mike August

Dave Dameshek

Paul Koehorst

Kevin Hench

Elliot Blut

Tall Jon

Jamie Agin

Anthony Carelli

Jack Mack

Toby Mergler

John Kasay

Bryan Paulk

Jim Brusca

Dan Dratch

Kristin Prouty

Lewis Kay

The Beast

Sean Desmond

Rachel Kambury

And finally, I'd like to thank whichever man, woman, or team of men and women finally figures out a vaccine for this shit-head virus.

I couldn't have done this without any of you, and I apologize for sullying your good names in the preceding pages.

—Pal Sal